DISCIPLINE
BEATS
VISION

HOW TO BE **THE LEADER** YOUR COMPANY NEEDS STARTING MONDAY

Dane Hudson

WILEY

First published 2026 by John Wiley & Sons Australia, Ltd

ISBN: 978-1-394-41463-5

A catalogue record for this book is available from the National Library of Australia

Registered Office
John Wiley & Sons Australia, Ltd. Level 4, 600 Bourke Street, Melbourne, VIC 3000, Australia

For details of our global editorial offices, customer services, and more information about Wiley products visit us at www.wiley.com.

Wiley also publishes its books in a variety of electronic formats and by print-on-demand. Some content that appears in standard print versions of this book may not be available in other formats.

Cover design by Wiley

Set in 11.5/15.5pts and Minion Pro by Straive, Chennai, India.
Printed and bound by CPI Group (UK) Ltd, Croydon, CR0 4YY
C9781394414635_070426

The manufacturer's authorized representative according to the EU General Product Safety Regulation is Wiley-VCH GmbH, Boschstr. 12, 69469 Weinheim, Germany, e-mail: Product_Safety@wiley.com.

For my wife, Melinda.
An extraordinary life partner and unwavering supporter through
more than 40 years of shared adventures — and still going.

Contents

Foreword

At some point in time, every CEO hits a performance wall. Somehow, the brilliant vision that carried their company this far seems to lose impact. Growth, profit and operational wins that once came easy become elusive, and the organisation loses momentum. In that moment, a good CEO asks urgent questions:

> *'Is the market changing?'*
> *'Is our strategy still relevant?'*
> *'Are our competitors outperforming us?'*
> *'Do my people have the skill sets to win?'*

These are all critical questions that require good answers. But, before tackling these questions, the best leaders I know typically ask a more important, and more difficult, question:

> *'Am I the leader my organisation needs right now?'*

By reaching for this book, *Discipline Beats Vision* by Dane Hudson, my guess is that you are now asking yourself this question. You know that a good look in the mirror is needed before you can solve your organisation's challenges. This question requires courage and humility, but it is the essential first step to breaking through your performance wall.

The good news delivered by *Discipline Beats Vision* is that you *can* be the leader your organisation needs if you are willing to put in the work. Dane Hudson's powerful book will show you how.

I've worked with many successful leaders during my career as a CEO, chairman, investor and management consultant. I've been CEO of John

Wiley & Sons, one of the world's largest publishers, a Senior Advisor for Providence Equity, President of Macmillan, Partner at LEK Consulting, and a division head at The Walt Disney Company. I've learned that the best CEOs have one common characteristic that powers sustained success. And contrary to the popular CEO-as-visionary narrative, it is not the brilliance of their vision. Instead, it is the consistency of their approach to leadership and management. In short, they've got a system, and they stick to it. And as Dane says, 'discipline beats vision' every time.

I've known Dane for several decades and have always admired his impressive career that rapidly took him from consultant to global CFO to winning CEO of several large and complex global organisations. While his results have always been stellar, even more impressive are his skills as a leader and mentor. In fact, Dane has long been on my short-list of advisors that I call for insights when I'm at the performance wall (see Chapter 7: Build your support team).

Several years ago, for example, I reached out to Dane for some advice. We were both leading large, global corporations at the time, and I was facing a thorny challenge that was inhibiting my company's progress. Specifically, the Company was at risk of being overwhelmed by increasing complexity as we adapted to rapid market changes and technological innovations.

As always, Dane listened, asked smart questions, and reflected back to me what he had heard along with potential solutions. Notably, he did not engage on mission, strategy or tactics. Instead, he challenged my focus, my leadership processes, and my team's culture. He suggested that improved process would create the capacity and produce big ideas, which they indeed did.

After the call, he sent me some pages outlining elements of the leadership program he had honed over his 20 years as a CEO. Included were examples of processes, communications and checklists that had helped him break through his own performance walls. For me, this was just what the doctor ordered, and it helped me adapt my style and better empower my team. Little did I know that these pages would be the foundation of *Discipline Beats Vision*.

A few years later, it was my turn to help Dane. He called just as his coaching firm, Impactful Leadership, was gaining momentum. He had quickly become one of the investment world's most in-demand CEO mentors. He asked me, as a publisher, if I thought there was a market need for a book on what he called 'disciplined leadership'. Knowing Dane and knowing publishing, my response was a definitive 'yes'.

My decades of work in publishing have given me a keen sense of what distinguishes a great leadership book from the thousands that get published each year. The book you now have in your hands succeeds by cutting through the noise to deliver a very big, somewhat contrarian idea — that discipline beats vision — and it delivers this message in a practical, step-by-step handbook that makes it easy to implement.

The big idea is simple: the key to driving long-term shareholder value creation is NOT the brilliance of a leader's vision; rather, it is the leader's consistent execution of a high-impact management program. Vision may set the direction, but discipline creates forward motion. Vision may tell us where we are going at first, but discipline enables rapid course correction when circumstances inevitably change.

Discipline Beats Vision will show you how to implement the powerful Impactful Leadership Framework. This is not classroom theory — it draws on Dane's proprietary 1000-page system of leadership tools, behaviours and templates refined in his years of being a successful CEO and his mentoring of over 150 founder CEOs. This framework has been battle-tested in boardrooms, crisis meetings and one-on-one sessions with leaders who needed results, not rhetoric.

Discipline Beats Vision practically demands to be acted upon. For example, Dane's signature 'Monday Ready' concept gives leaders a built-in mechanism for instigating real behavioural change. Every chapter ends with a simple challenge: don't wait for the perfect plan; change one thing this Monday. This bias to action ensures that the time between thinking and doing — the gap that plagues so many transformations — is bridged immediately.

Discipline Beats Vision is timely, practical and impactful. It will equip leaders of all stripes with the toolkit to build great teams that turn vision into results. Read it carefully, apply it consistently, and *Discipline Beats Vision* will help you break through your performance wall to become the leader your organisation needs and deserves — beginning on Monday.

Brian Napack
Brian Napack is a recognised leader in education, scientific research and publishing. His impact-driven career includes successful tenures as CEO of John Wiley & Sons, President of Macmillan, Senior Advisor at Providence Equity, Partner at LEK Consulting, and head of Disney Education at The Walt Disney Company. He is currently Executive Chairman of 2U, Inc and serves as an active investor, director and advisor for multiple companies in media, education and science.

Introduction

Let me start with a simple, contrarian truth:
discipline beats vision

Vision is important. It's what drives you as a leader, inspires your team, attracts investors, and is the basis for your optimism when you launch a business. But vision without discipline is powerless, as it is simply a targeted destination. I am sure many of you have heard the quote 'Hope is not a strategy'. Well your *vision* is your hope, and *discipline* is the vehicle, the fuel and the roadmap that will get you there.

What separates leaders who scale from those who don't isn't a bolder vision — it's their disciplined leadership behaviours that turn vision into reality.

So, what do I mean by *disciplined leadership*?

Firstly, it is being *deliberate*: deliberate in how you lead yourself; deliberate in the behaviours you use to build trust and accountability, and develop your team; deliberate in how you lead your board rather than being led by them; and deliberate and determined in how you handle and learn from setbacks and crises. Being a disciplined leader means executing the right choices constantly and consistently, even when they are uncomfortable or inconvenient. Disciplined leadership means understanding the outcome you want and then *deliberately* demonstrating the behaviours that you know will deliver your desired outcomes. If you want to achieve your vision, you cannot leave any of these areas to chance.

Secondly, it is having the *awareness* and understanding that every one of your actions, such as what you say, who you speak to, how you react to a situation, even your calendar, is being watched and judged, and has an immediate impact on the people you lead and on the organisation. Even a subtle gesture by you is exaggerated by your role as founder CEO. The team also copies you, so what you do and how you lead sets the example and is multiplied throughout the organisation. For this reason you must be a *role model* of your own and the company's *values* and for what you expect from your team. Disciplined leaders use this positional power to their advantage to embed a culture that aligns with the company's values and demonstrates how they want their team to lead. The term for this is your *leadership shadow*, and we introduce this concept in Chapter 2 then reinforce it in almost every subsequent chapter.

Finally, disciplined leaders are never satisfied with their own capabilities and continue to grow themselves as leaders. They do this because they realise that if they do not scale their leadership competencies then the business won't scale either. You may see this as a paradox because discipline may suggest rigidity. However, disciplined leaders are *relentless students*. They invest not just in their businesses but in themselves, always investing and expanding their skills and even reinventing themselves when that is needed.

Disciplined leader summary

Disciplined leaders are deliberate and self-aware, and consistently role-model the behaviours they expect from others. They are relentless students, constantly evolving their leadership approaches and reinventing themselves as new challenges arise or as the business requires.

This book is not leadership theory. Instead it is about the *every-moment behaviours* that move you towards becoming an outstanding leader. It is written with founder CEOs in mind; those who have already built strong products, gained sales traction and are scaling their teams. But disciplined leadership is not just for founders. Whether you are running a multi-billion-dollar company, leading a family business, or stepping into your first leadership role, the principles here apply equally. Disciplined leadership is industry-agnostic and stage-agnostic. The insights you'll find here are designed to help you wherever you are on your leadership journey.

To scale your business you must evolve your leadership

If you are a founder CEO, let me start by acknowledging that you've done something remarkable. Your business has grown beyond its early 'garage days', and you are now leading a mid-to-large team. You have secured funding, your product is gaining real market traction, and you are likely to be expanding internationally.

You are also now realising that the leadership skills that brought you here won't take you where you want to go. There are now significant challenges in the business that you have never encountered before. Compounding this are other factors, for example you may be newly married, possibly with children. You might struggle to navigate these challenges separately, let alone when they interplay with each other, and you're also struggling to manage the stress this puts on you.

I have seen this over and over again, having been a CEO myself for 25 years in multiple industries and in many different countries, and having mentored more than 150 CEOs on their journeys.

The first concept I address when working with my clients is to help them recognise that the phrase 'People are born leaders' is a myth. Instead, it is a person's life journey and how they leverage those learnings that creates their leadership skills. Often, so-called 'born leaders' had parents who nurtured them as leaders, gave them a voice at the dinner table, and encouraged them to have confidence in their abilities. At other times 'born leaders' were simply bigger or a bit smarter than their peers, and so were placed into positions of leadership where they had to learn and adjust to this extra responsibility.

Outstanding leaders are *relentless students*, knowing that their learning journey can never stop. They also know that an inspiring vision of what they are creating is necessary to build an amazing company, but is not sufficient to drive the team and the organisation to that goal. What separates those who scale from those who fail is the discipline in how they lead — the deliberate, consistent and repeatable behaviours that build trust, instil accountability, shape a deliberate company culture and help to navigate through crises.

Outstanding leadership is something you evolve into as new challenges arise that you overcome and you learn from. The word 'evolve' is deliberately chosen. Your current leadership capabilities are likely already strong — they have brought you this far and enabled your business to scale to this point. *But evolution is required to move you from where you are today to the leader your company needs tomorrow.* It's not about a dramatic reinvention, but about being more deliberate in your leadership behaviours.

This is why discipline beats vision. Your vision for the company is inspiring you and the team, but it is your evolution into a more consistent and disciplined leader that will turn that vision into reality.

Much like those young people who were suddenly thrust into leadership roles and had to grow into them, you too have found yourself in a position where others now look to you for motivation and guidance. Your intellect, intuition and technical talent may have taken the business this far, but scaling it further demands more. Becoming truly outstanding as a leader requires deliberate investment in yourself and an evolution in how you lead.

As your company scales, the bottleneck almost always becomes your leadership: your self-awareness; your communication skills; your ability to motivate, empower and develop your team; and your ability to pivot, restructure and relaunch when the market shifts and new challenges arise. If you are not a *relentless student*, your company stops growing. Just as you continue to improve your technical or engineering skills to enhance your product, the same investment is required constantly in extending your leadership skills.

As a mentor, I try to demystify leadership. It should not be viewed as an ambiguous concept. Consider Isaac Newton's Third Law of Motion, 'For every action, there is an equal and opposite reaction'. Disciplined leadership is the same. Your actions as a leader will generate a response from your team. To become an impactful and outstanding leader you need to know what outcome you are targeting from your team and then execute behaviours to elicit that response from them. This is a learned practical skill that must be authentic and become a habit. Vision will inspire the team to head in a direction towards your company's grand goal, but your disciplined leadership is required to build an integrated team that works as one, overcoming challenges and moving the business forward. Every leadership behaviour you demonstrate as CEO triggers a response from your team but the real question here is — Are you aware and disciplined enough to ensure that the response you get is the one you want?

The optimism trap that may be sabotaging your success

As a scaling founder CEO, you face a dangerous paradox. The same optimism and vision that launched your company risks derailing it. You cannot build a company without massive optimism — it's essential for convincing investors, attracting talent and persevering through setbacks. But that optimism is unfounded without disciplined leadership. Optimism can even become a trap if it blinds you to critical leadership gaps that compound as you scale.

It is not the founder with the boldest vision who succeeds, but the one who applies disciplined leadership behaviours, every day.

I've seen this pattern repeatedly across Asia, Australia and beyond. Brilliant founders with large teams, significant funding and market momentum hit invisible walls. These CEOs work 18-hour days for some, if not all, of the reasons below:

- They need to resolve operational and customer issues as they scale a product that is just shy of where it needs to be, but feel there is no time to fix it.
- They need to build strong functional teams in areas where they have limited knowledge, so there is a lot of trial and error.
- They micromanage talented people, involving themselves in every decision.
- They need to wear multiple hats as their key team members — having become frustrated by the CEO's undisciplined approach to leading the business — depart.
- They struggle with balancing the three major stakeholders in their lives — the business, the investors/board, and their own families — all of whom get frustrated with the lack of focus on their needs and the lack of time spent with each of them.

The technical skills and product vision that led to your initial success in the business cannot solve the complex leadership challenges of scaling up from a team of ten people to twenty, to hundreds, and then to thousands. The statistics are sobering; the Australian Bureau of Statistics in 2023 confirmed that 48 percent of new businesses fail within four years. Similarly, US statistics confirm 45 percent of new registered companies fail by year five. I am certain the percentage is considerably higher as many companies fail before even registering the business. In my experience, failure rarely stems from not having a bold vision or even issues finding product–market fit, it comes from the leader's inability to evolve from a specialist, such as an engineer, to a disciplined leader.

Foundation for the handbook

Discipline Beats Vision is distilled from my 25 years of CEO experience, mentoring more than 150 CEOs, and creating a 1000-page leadership framework, known as the Impactful Leadership Framework. What took me decades to learn through trial and error, you can master in months and at a fraction of the cost of any formal business education.

This handbook will provide you with recommendations on impactful leadership behaviours and give you tools and frameworks that will support you on your leadership growth to successfully scale the business. By using this book you will be able to identify the changes you need to make in leading your team. Initially some of your changes may feel awkward or unnatural; however, I promise that with time these new leadership behaviours will become habits and will become natural for you, as they did for me.

This handbook is targeted at founder CEOs with more than 100 employees. Yet, as mentioned earlier, the principles apply just as powerfully to any leader who wants to sharpen their leadership discipline. The handbook represents something unique: real-world leadership education about practical leadership behaviours that deliver immediate results.

Monday ready

As a call to action through each chapter, I use the concept of *Monday ready* — it's a challenge to you to immediately apply key learnings and implement leadership behavioural changes, starting Monday. This concept comes from my days as a consultant, when I was trained to always ask, 'So what?' What is the underlying message in the data? What's the takeaway for the client? And what should they do differently? As you reflect on each chapter's insights, do your own 'So what?' analysis and make the deliberate decision to introduce more leadership discipline into how you lead *on Monday*.

To prompt you in identifying your biggest opportunity areas, the following are provided in the book:

1. Personal leadership assessment. The next chapter is a simple assessment for you to evaluate your strengths and your likely opportunity areas. Use this as a compass to direct you to the relevant chapter which covers your biggest areas of opportunity.
2. Founder stories that provide real-world examples to strengthen a concept or idea. At the end of each of these stories, I pose a question, a *Monday reflection*, to prompt you to consider doing something different in how you lead, *starting Monday*.
3. Chapter summaries. At the end of each chapter, there is a chapter summary for you to list what you will start doing (or do more of) and what you may stop doing (or do less of), starting Monday.

How to use this handbook

This handbook is designed for easy navigation. The following are some suggestions for how to get the most from it:

1. **Start with Chapters 1 and 2**
   While this handbook is flexible, I strongly recommend you begin in Chapter 1 with the personal leadership assessment, as this will direct you to your biggest areas of opportunity. Then, regardless of your results, move on to Chapter 2 where the key characteristics and responsibilities of impactful leaders are introduced — a critical foundation for you as a leader and one that gives you context for making sense of the chapters that follow.
2. **This is not a linear manual: identify your biggest growth areas first**
   It's built for the messy, dynamic reality of leading a scaling business. Each chapter stands alone and addresses a specific leadership challenge. Use the self-assessment in Chapter 1 to

pinpoint where your leadership opportunities are. Prioritise chapters that speak directly to those. Your time is probably limited, so focus on areas where the return will be highest.

3. **Don't try to do everything**

   This handbook is deliberately comprehensive and dense with content around very specific actions and behaviours that you can implement immediately. Take what's useful for you now, and don't feel pressure to apply it all at once. Think of it as a resource you'll return to again and again.

4. **Adapt the tools to your context**

   The frameworks and behaviours shared are proven, but they still need to be translated into your leadership style, team dynamics, and the company's stage of growth. Some concepts may feel too advanced for where your company is today. That's okay. Put them aside for later.

5. **Learn from fellow leaders**

   Each chapter includes Founder stories. While I do share many of my own stories to explain concepts in the book, I realise that my stories can have a bias towards bigger companies, so I also share stories from my clients working in smaller enterprises. This brings their stories, and the lessons they learned, to life and also shows how others, like you, have tackled similar challenges.

6. **Leverage the templates**

   In almost every chapter I provide templates that you may find useful in your business.

7. **Do something different on Monday!**

   As mentioned earlier, this book was written to inspire you to act now. Each chapter finishes with a summary of key messages and challenges you to identify what you will do differently as a leader on Monday, encouraging you to move from a passive reader of this book to being a practician, using these new leadership behaviours.

Although I encourage you to flip through the book and focus on the topics most relevant to your leadership growth, this handbook is intentionally structured to mirror the stages of a scaling business, helping you anticipate and prepare for the challenges leaders most often face at each stage.

Chapters 1 and 2 lay the foundation for disciplined leadership, showing you how to connect your personal journey with your role as CEO. You'll learn what outstanding leadership looks like, explore your key responsibilities, and understand the concept of the 'shadow of the leader', which will surface in nearly every chapter of the book.

Chapters 3 to 6 guide you on the leadership levers you pull daily to build a strong team and sustainable business. These chapters show you how to raise trust levels, create an accountable and deliberate culture, grow your team, and communicate with impact. These four chapters provide the most powerful leadership behaviours to guide your team and organisation and thereby turn your inspirational vision into reality and results.

Chapter 7 shows you that, just as a professional tennis player has a comprehensive team to support them on their journey, you need to intentionally design an evolving support network for the many different stages of your professional and life journey.

Chapters 8 and 9 prepare you for the complexity that comes when your business has scaled considerably, with you now bringing in a board and expanding overseas. You'll learn how to maintain control of your company's direction by managing your board and investors with disciplined practices, and how to lead teams across borders, navigate cultural differences and build a sustainable international operation.

Chapter 10 equips you with the tools to handle the personal side of leadership, leveraging both grit and resilience to enable you to stay grounded and impactful under pressure.

Responding to the cynics

Some readers will glance through this book and point to very successful, high-profile outliers like Elon Musk or Steve Jobs, and think that they don't look much like the disciplined leader described in this book. These readers might be commenting on:

- **Self-awareness.** Both leaders have been portrayed as being indifferent to how they are viewed — or at least unconcerned by it.
- **Role modelling.** Neither fits the conventional balanced, respectful, role model template.
- **Values in action.** It is hard to see this come through consistently given the chaotic and aggressive way they both at times seemed to lead.

My response is that while Musk may appear unconcerned with some traditional leadership approaches, he is *highly deliberate* in how he leads and is a *relentless student*, as evidenced by the innovation in creating SpaceX and Tesla. And Jobs also aligned himself with the disciplined leader model in that he knew discipline beats vision! In his second stint as CEO of Apple he knew where he wanted to take the company and the products to get there. He then demonstrated intense *discipline* with deliberate and maniacal focus on innovation, customer centricity, product quality and distribution. Both these leaders had truly inspiring visions for their businesses but knew it was only through disciplined and deliberate leadership they could achieve their ultimate goals.

With that said, there is no guarantee that being a disciplined leader, who is *deliberate, self-aware, value-based*, a *role model* and a *relentless student*, will lead to you building a unicorn. But it materially increases the odds that your vision will become a reality, and that you can scale it without burning out your team or yourself.

It's time to achieve your vision through discipline

You have a bold vision and likely have already proven you can build something significant. Now it's time to prove you can scale it to the size that achieves your ultimate goal. The difference between the leaders who achieve their ambitious vision and those who plateau is more than your aspirational vision of the market opportunity and the quality of your product or service — it's discipline. Discipline is the *how*.

Your optimism and vision got you here. But discipline will get you where you want to go. By embracing the habits and behaviours in this handbook, you won't just be a visionary founder, you'll become a disciplined, impactful leader, Monday after Monday.

CHAPTER 1

Personal leadership assessment

A ll CEOs like to measure what matters. Measurement gives us a clear benchmark for where we are today, and a way to track our progress over time. We are also competitive, so once we see a score we naturally want to improve it.

This chapter provides a set of focused questions to evaluate where you currently stand against the leadership disciplines and behaviours that turn vision into results. I have used this tool nearly 100 times with clients and find that it's consistently powerful for identifying the biggest opportunities for personal growth. In practice, I combine the leader's self-assessment with interviews with the key people around them, and this often reveals blind spots that the leaders themselves cannot see.

As you read through the questions — and the chapters — you may feel there is a bias towards big companies and think that they may not all be relevant to a smaller startup. My response is that the only sections that may not be relevant are Chapter 8 on board management, and Chapter 9 on leading international businesses, as your company may not be there yet. The remainder of the chapters and questions are relevant whether you have ten people on your team or 10 000.

The leadership assessment survey

For the most accurate picture, complete this assessment with a critical and candid perspective. To do this, use the template in table 1.1 (overleaf) and the scoring guide following the template.

Table 1.1 The leadership survey template

		Score (1–5)
Personal leadership discipline (Ch. 2)		
1	Are you disciplined in how you lead your business — calm, organised, punctual and proactive?	
2	Do you see yourself as an effective leader, measured by your impact in moving the team and the organisation towards your company's vision?	
3	Do you know your CEO responsibilities beyond product building and sales?	
4	Do you deliberately and consistently execute all of your CEO responsibilities?	
5	Do you understand the power of your leadership shadow and deliberately use it to set the tone for your team?	
Trust and accountability (Ch. 3)		
6	Do you know how to build trust across your team and organisation?	
7	Are you skilled and confident in constructively handling difficult conversations and managing conflict?	
8	Does your company have a culture where accountability is the norm, and commitments are consistently delivered?	
9	When accountability gaps appear, do you know which levers to pull to fix the issue?	
Company culture (Ch. 4)		
10	Do you have a clear and memorable vision, purpose and set of values?	
11	Can 70% of your organisation recite them?	
12	Are your values consistently used as filters for the organisation's decision making?	
13	Is your team's behaviour aligned with those values every day?	
14	Can you articulate the company's culture?	
15	Do you use recognition as a tool to motivate the team?	
Team development (Ch. 5)		
16	Do you and your team do annual performance appraisals?	
17	Do you have a structured approach to developing your leaders?	

		Score (1–5)
18	Are your best people developing and being promoted — or are they leaving for other opportunities?	
19	Do you actively mentor and grow high-potential talent?	
20	Do you have a mechanism to receive honest feedback on your own leadership performance?	

Communication (Ch. 6)

21	Are you a confident and persuasive communicator in all settings — one-on-ones, team meetings, board meetings, investor presentations?	
22	Do you regularly (at least once a month) hold all-hands meetings with the majority, if not all of the organisation?	
23	In times of crisis, do you know how to rally and energise your team?	

Board management (Ch. 8)

24	Are you comfortable — with minimal anxiety — working with boards and investors?	
25	Do you lead board meetings with clarity and discipline rather than being led by the board?	
26	Are you leveraging their expertise and network to accelerate your business?	

Leading international businesses (Ch. 9)

27	Are you clear on your growth approach in each international market?	
28	Have you built competent, trusted local leadership teams?	
29	Do the international businesses exhibit the same culture as the home/local market? If not, do you know how to remedy this?	
30	Are you confident your international operations are fully compliant with local and global regulations?	

Personal sustainability (Ch. 7 and 10)

31	In a crisis, do you feel centred and in control?	
32	Are you resilient, maintaining calm and consistent leadership under stress?	

(*continued*)

Table 1.1 (continued)

		Score (1–5)
33	Do you invest in your own leadership journey through mentors, coaches and support networks?	
34	Is your work–life integration healthy — and does your partner agree?	
35	Are you a role model for discipline and balance, both at work and at home?	

How to score yourself

For each question, rate yourself on a scale of 1 to 5.

1 = Never/Not at all
2 = Occasionally, with significant room for improvement
3 = Neutral
4 = Often, and generally satisfied with performance
5 = Always/Consistently excellent

I would encourage you to try not to use the score of 3. Instead, use a 2 or 4 as this will assist in directing you to your areas of opportunity.

There are 35 questions so a perfect total score would be 175, but any total over 140 is very good as it suggests a score of 4 or higher to almost every question. So, calculate your total score and then set it to one side. Instead of looking at your total score I encourage you to focus your attention on analysing your scores in each section.

If you have clusters of scores of 1 and 2, and no 4s or 5s in a section, then that is an area of opportunity. It clearly identifies where you should prioritise your focus when using this book. To assist, I have labelled the relevant chapters in each section.

Good luck on your journey to lift your score and, more importantly, become a disciplined leader who will translate your company's vision into reality through impactful leadership behaviours.

CHAPTER 2

Translate your life journey into your leadership journey

Becoming an outstanding and impactful leader involves recognising that your life's journey, including all your personal and career experiences, is your leadership growth journey. Becoming a disciplined leader requires you to become a *relentless student* by investing time to observe, reflect and evolve your leadership behaviours into powerful levers to guide your team and the business. The word *evolve* is used deliberately, because you are a leader today and already have a leadership style and behaviours that are entrenched; to change these will take time and targeted effort.

Disciplined leadership — along with the vision for your company — does not just happen. Becoming a great leader results from you investing in this journey by observing other leaders, researching outstanding leaders, reflecting on your own leadership style, and receiving mentoring or coaching, then figuring out what is working and what is not, and changing accordingly. This is the work needed for you to make your vision a reality. Once you know what disciplined and impactful leadership looks like, you can determine which behaviours you can authentically copy from outstanding leaders and which you can't.

Early in my career I aspired to be a great leader. One thing I did early on was create an Excel spreadsheet in which I wrote down the characteristics of every boss I worked for and of others who were senior in the company. I made a note of the leadership traits that made a positive impact, as well as those that didn't and which instead demotivated or confused me. I did this over a 15-year period, and this helped me learn what outstanding leadership looked and felt like, through my own experiences of being impacted by those leaders. There is a great quote: 'People rarely remember the exact words you say, but they always remember how you made them feel'. My spreadsheet was biased towards behaviours with this quote in mind.

This practice became foundational to my leadership growth and is why I now encourage my clients to become *students of leadership*. Not necessarily with a spreadsheet, but with a deliberate system that forces them to observe, reflect and authentically copy impactful behaviours. It is this discipline, not vision, that ensures those observations turn into habits.

In this chapter, we will go deeper into understanding how you can invest in your leadership journey. I will share the ten characteristics that disciplined impactful leaders show; then introduce and explain the important concept of your *leadership shadow*; and finally, highlight the nine responsibilities of outstanding leaders.

Invest in your leadership journey

Let's start with a question: Are you willing to dedicate your time, attention and resources to becoming a disciplined and outstanding leader?

If the answer is yes, then this handbook will assist you on the journey. To be an outstanding leader you must be a *relentless student* and deliberately invest in your leadership journey. Just as you would invest time in learning a new technical skill, a language or a musical instrument, you need to be deliberate in using your life journey to accumulate learnings for your leadership growth. Observe leaders in action, reflect on their impact on yourself or others, and then copy and evolve your own authentic leadership style.

You may be thinking at this point, 'I'm a good leader today and I don't have time to do this. I'm extremely busy dealing with challenges across my team and the complexity of scaling the business'.

My response is that you are a good leader today — you would not have built your business to more than 100 people if that was not the case. However, to build a business of significant size you must become an outstanding leader. Just as driving your business forward to meet your vision takes time, focus and resources, your personal growth also requires you to invest in building impactful leadership behaviours and skills.

How can you take action?

Refer to figure 2.1. It's called a *leadership lifeline*. Each box represents one of the five people who have most shaped you as a leader. Over the years, I've asked hundreds of leaders to complete this exercise, and interestingly — although not surprisingly — the people most commonly identified are one or both parents.

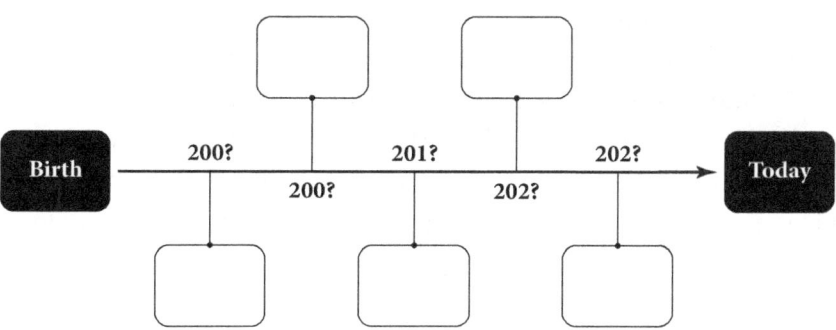

Figure 2.1 Leadership lifeline

Consider how you would fill in the chart yourself. For each person identified, ask yourself these three questions.

1. **Why did this person affect you?** For example, if you chose your mother, was it because she gave you constructive feedback that helped guide you when you were uncertain about the way forward? If it was your first boss, why did they stand out versus other bosses?

2. **What characteristics did they exhibit?** For instance, your mother may have been a role model with a calm presence, managing a full-time job while always being available to help and guide you. If it was your first boss, it may have been their clarity in identifying the root cause of problems in the business and being able to communicate that with simplicity.

3. **How does this connect to your leadership today?** Reflect on whether you are consciously, or subconsciously, copying any of the traits you identified above. Chances are, you are.

Importantly, your list should include both positive and negative influences. Ineffective or even aggressive leaders often leave just as strong an imprint, shaping what you *don't* want to replicate.

By doing this leadership lifeline exercise you will notice that you've unconsciously adopted some of the positive behaviours you have observed in others. What I encourage you to do from now on is to be deliberate in observing both great and poor leadership. Identify how a leader *makes you feel* — that's the best way to gauge their impact. Then identify which impactful behaviours you can *authentically copy*.

Let me give you an example. Most people reading this book will have heard of Sir Richard Branson, the UK-based entrepreneur who started Virgin Music, Virgin Airlines and many other businesses. One thing that I had read about him was his ability and deliberate approach to enter an event in a very noticeable, significant way to make it memorable for the audience. When Branson launched his first space flight with Virgin Galactic, and on which he was a passenger, he rode a bike from his hotel to the launch site. Someone videoed this and shared it with the media. It brilliantly connects one of the oldest (bicycle) and newest (rocket ship) forms of transport. Thereby it made the launch even more memorable.

The example I want to share of me authentically copying occurred when my previous company held an event in Singapore at which I was hosting a crowd of 600. I dressed up as a lion to perform a lion dance — which is a part of Chinese culture around Chinese New Year. I did the lion dance up the centre aisle with our Singapore Country Manager. It took around five minutes and was an energetic dance up the aisle to the stage. Once on stage, the Singapore Country Manager and I both took off our lion heads to the cheers of the crowd, as they had not known it was us. Was this showing off? No, it was a way to create a truly memorable start for the 600 attendees. Even eight years later, when I reconnected with people who were at the event, they vividly remembered that moment kicking off the conference. This is a great example of identifying a powerful leadership behaviour that I observed in another leader, and which I could authentically copy.

Monday reflection

Think about the leaders you respect, either from your timeline or a leader you have read about. Is there a behaviour you could authentically copy that would have a positive impact *on* your business?

The top ten leadership characteristics

Leadership **characteristics** describe *who you are as a leader* — your inherent style, your mindset, and the way you show up in front of others. The characteristics are visible in how you speak, the way you listen, your approach to making decisions, and how you interact with your team day-to-day. Characteristics are important for many reasons, including the impact they have on the company's culture, and can shape how people feel when they work with you. In reflecting on the disciplined leader definition, your leadership characteristics play a significant role in exhibiting *self-awareness, values and role modelling,* and in setting the standard for your team.

An output from your leadership lifeline should be a list of what you have identified as powerful leadership characteristics, either from the people who influenced you or from your own experiences. My learning, hopefully validated by your reflections, is that impactful leaders share a common set of characteristics. Below, I share the leadership traits that describe how disciplined and impactful leaders behave and operate every moment of every day.

1. A disciplined leader is a person of hope

I love action movies, and one of my all-time favourites is *Gladiator* with Russell Crowe. In the film, Crowe portrays Maximus Aurelius, a Roman army general who suffers betrayal and ends up as a gladiator. When he was a general, people followed him out of duty and because of respect for his title. But once he became a gladiator, he was just another fighter — no rank, no official authority. Yet people still followed him. Why? Because he gave them hope. His confidence in battle and in directing the other gladiators gave them a reason to believe that they could survive, and even win.

In your business, people follow you not because of your title, but because they have confidence and believe in you. They choose to work for you when they have other options. And while there may be many reasons they stay; the most fundamental one is that they believe in you, and believe that your leadership can take the business towards its vision. You are a person of hope for them.

Reflecting on the book title, *Discipline Beats Vision,* this is an example of the power of having an inspiring vision. However, the team will only stay if they believe you have the ability and discipline to drive the business to that destination.

Founder story

Janice experienced a profound change in 2022 and 2023 as she struggled to obtain funding, with venture capital (VC) funds rapidly turning their focus away from revenue growth to profitability. This required her to pivot and significantly downsize her team.

One of the most difficult times to be a 'person of hope' is when you have to reduce your team by 20 or 30 per cent. Janice had to do exactly that. To remain a person of hope, and to energise her team, she acted quickly.

Over one day she dismissed 15 people — which was 20 per cent of her team. That afternoon she quickly connected with the remainder of the organisation in an all-hands Zoom call. The messaging was short and simple:

'It was sad and disappointing to have to let go a number of good people today. The reason for this was that three of our products are taking longer to generate material levels of revenue. We have plenty of funds in the bank but need to be cautious in how we spend that. So we decided to put these products on hold, and as a consequence the people working on those products were let go.

'Our remaining business is strong. We have sales momentum and great potential, so that is where we will focus. Regardless of the restructuring today, I remain extremely optimistic about the future of our company. We are not planning any more restructuring, although I don't have a crystal ball, so we all need to continue to look after our customers. If any of you have concerns, please come and talk to me'.

(continued)

The next morning she met with the ten people who were the superstars in the business and reassured them about the future. She met them one-on-one.

This approach and messaging worked. She did lose one or two people who were concerned but the large majority of the organisation quickly bounced back and focused on the business because, even with the restructuring, they believed in Janice.

Monday reflection

Are you a 'person of hope' at least 90 *per cent* of the time, including in tough times like the above? If not, what can you do differently on Monday to increase that percentage?

2. Disciplined leaders must be simplifiers

Impactful leaders have a unique ability: they can take a complex situation, process the details, and articulate the problem, its root cause, and the actions required in a clear, concise manner. It's not that they see things differently from others — it's that they can distil complexity into clarity. They have a concise and coherent way of communicating.

However, be cautious. Simplifying the problem is one thing, but that doesn't mean the solution itself is simple. The key to success in this area is to refine your ability to listen actively, absorb multiple perspectives, narrow all the information down into what is truly the issue and then communicate in a way that makes sense to your team. I promise that this is a skill that improves with deliberate practice — first listen intently, focusing only on what is being said, then ask questions for insight into the core issue, pay attention to how you frame problems and choose your words wisely.

3. Disciplined leaders are purpose-driven

People don't just work for a company; they work to support the company to deliver on its purpose and vision. They want to feel connected to something bigger than themselves. Consider Steve Jobs, the late founder of Apple. His passion and purpose were to create meaningful, beautifully designed products. His obsessive and disciplined focus, and unwavering belief in his vision defined him. Another example is Henry Ford, who famously said, 'If I had asked customers what they wanted, they would have said faster horses'. Both leaders had an unshakable ambition to not just redefine their industries, but to change people's lives.

As the leader of your business, your everyday actions must reinforce the vision and the purpose of the company.

Founder story

Two different founders I know are building companies that are creating a more sustainable world. One of them is reconditioning school buses to move from being petrol-powered to electric vehicles, while the other is using solar panels to power irrigation pumps across small farms in Southeast Asia. Both these businesses have purposes which inspire their teams.

These companies, because of their products, are in the perfect position to create a powerful purpose. However, I would suggest that most companies can create a stronger purpose.

Monday reflection

As the leader, have you created a strong purpose for your business? If not, then it is time to do so, on Monday.

Your responsibility is to inspire your team by demonstrating your own passion and commitment. People will rally behind you if they see that your ambition is genuine, and your purpose is clear and aligned with their own value system.

4. Disciplined leaders are role models

Leaders must be role models. I'll keep repeating this throughout this book because it's that important. Your team is always watching you. They listen to what you say but, more importantly, they observe what you do. They will mirror your behaviours, your values and even your energy level. For example, when you are in the office the energy level is higher; if it isn't, you need to ramp things up.

And if they don't respect the way you lead, they will leave. I've been there. l spent six years working for a top-tier consulting firm and was close to making partner but I decided to leave. Why? Because when I looked at the partners I saw few role models. I didn't aspire to become like them. That realisation was enough for me to walk away.

In the following chapters I will be specific about the deliberate behaviours you can adopt to ensure your role modelling has the desired impact on your team and the organisation.

5. Disciplined leaders are respectful

Whether you are speaking to another CEO or the person who cleans your office, show them the same level of respect. Leadership is a privilege, not a right. It doesn't make you better than anyone else, it simply gives you the opportunity to serve others in a meaningful way.

True respect is about valuing people for who they are. When you treat everyone with dignity, you create a culture where people feel valued and motivated to do their best work.

You have no doubt heard of the golden rule: 'Treat people how you want to be treated'. I read once about the platinum rule: 'Treat people how they want to be treated'. This requires you to have either strong emotional intelligence or simply be good at asking questions. An example is when one of your team members wants to be given a target and then allowed to go after it. Alternatively, another team member may require 15 minutes with you to brainstorm different task completion methods and confirm their understanding of the specifications. This is an example of treating people with respect and leading them in a way that works best for them.

6. Disciplined leaders are empowering

What do you do when a team member comes to you with a question? Do you immediately give them the answer? If so, you are training them to rely on you rather than think for themselves. Once you start doing this, it is unlikely to stop.

Instead, challenge them. Ask, 'What would you do' or 'What would you suggest?' If they don't have an answer, encourage them to return with potential solutions. This shift in approach puts the responsibility back on the team member to think independently and empowers them to take ownership of their decisions. Over time, they will stop bringing you problems and start bringing well thought out solutions.

With the above said, you do not have to accept their suggestion. You are still in charge and may say, 'Good suggestion. However, I think maybe a better approach this time is…' Use this as a teaching moment for them.

A phrase to remember here to prompt you to lead in an empowering way is, 'Don't make decisions for others'.

7. Disciplined leaders speak last

The moment a CEO speaks, their opinion becomes the dominant one in the room. Even in organisations that promote open discussion, once the leader shares their perspective, it influences the direction of the conversation. In some cultures, particularly in Asia, the team is very hierarchical and deferential, so challenging a CEO's viewpoint can be rare.

To encourage honest dialogue and better decision making, a CEO should make it a habit to listen first and speak last. An approach to do this is to describe the issue, providing the team context, then work your way around the room (or Zoom call gallery) asking each person their opinion, prior to providing your own. You do not need to take the majority view; it is still your final decision.

This is an area where most of my clients initially struggle, as they feel it is their responsibility as the founder CEO to lead the discussion, including giving their opinion upfront.

A prompt to keep this top of mind is that you are endeavouring to make each member of your team a key participant in building the business, as opposed to a passenger simply on the ride!

Monday reflection

Are you the last to provide an opinion in team meetings? Can you change that, starting *on* Monday?

8. Disciplined leaders trust their gut

Anticipate, so you are not forced into making urgent decisions. Trust your gut and instincts. If something feels off, it probably is. One of the most common mistakes I see leaders make is waiting too long to act, particularly with decisions about people.

I've learned the hard way that I tend to fire people about nine months too late. I usually know they aren't the right fit long before

I act, but I hesitate out of loyalty. My advice to you? If your gut tells you something isn't right — whether it's an employee, a customer or the financial performance of a division — act sooner rather than later.

A common example with customers is that you are waiting for the response regarding a tender, or you have put a proposal in to renew a contract; however, the customer's response is slower than you expect. You have a gut sense that something is wrong. In this situation, call them; your gut is probably right.

9. Disciplined leaders have confidence with humility

Confidence is essential for leadership, your team needs to see you as decisive and feel secure in your decision making and ability to lead. There is, however, a fine line between self-assurance and arrogance, and crossing that line can erode trust within your team.

Outstanding leaders are confident in their abilities but remain humble enough to listen, learn and adapt. They recognise that leadership is not about being the smartest person in the room but about fostering an environment where the best ideas come forward. They also have the confidence to admit when they are wrong.

Another concept that is similar to humility is vulnerability. Impactful leaders, at times, also need to show their vulnerability; show they are human and that they also have feelings and emotions.

10. Leaders are relentless students and are able to reinvent themselves

An absolutely critical element of being a disciplined leader is being a *relentless student*. People often cite curiosity as an essential trait of outstanding leaders, and for good reason. The world changes rapidly, and leadership demands continuous learning. What worked for you last year may not work for you next year. As your business scales, your leadership must evolve with it.

We discussed earlier the importance of your leadership journey — being intentional about researching, observing, reflecting and adapting. Disciplined leaders never stop learning. They embrace change and seek new perspectives, and will reinvent themselves.

I would like to think that this last characteristic is one that I routinely role-model. I have been a CEO in five different industries, which shows my nimbleness and ability to learn. However, something I share with my clients is that one of the reasons I could do this is my ability to see the similarities in how these industries operated. As a result, I was able to use my toolkit of leadership, strategic and operational skills to shorten the learning curve. An example is that the approach to sell to large enterprise businesses is very similar, no matter what the product or service is. A *relentless student* is always adding to their leadership toolkit.

In summary, below are the ten characteristics I believe define disciplined and impactful leaders who turn their vision into reality.

1. Person of hope
2. Simplifier
3. Purpose-driven
4. Role model
5. Respectful
6. Empowering
7. Trusts their gut
8. Speaks last
9. Confident with humility
10. Relentless learner.

After reviewing this list, I suggest you consider two things: first, whether you agree with this list. If you do, then assess yourself honestly — how well do you embody these traits in your own leadership? If you disagree, then create your own list and commit to showing those qualities more frequently and consistently in how you lead.

As I mentioned in number ten above, leadership is not static — it's a lifelong journey of growth and refinement. Keep this list handy and regularly reflect on whether, and how well, you are displaying these characteristics.

Use your leadership shadow for good, not evil

A CEO's 'leadership shadow' is the powerful influence that their behaviours, decisions and communication style have on the entire organisation. Whether intentional or not, your team will mirror what you model. How you act becomes the blueprint for how others lead, decide and behave.

Your leadership shadow is arguably your most impactful leadership lever. Every behaviour you exhibit affects your team and the organisation. You need to understand how to optimise and use your shadow to create a positive impact, as opposed to a negative or neutral impact.

Let me give you an example of how powerful a CEO's leadership shadow can be. Early in my career, I worked for a company in Australia. The company had just started a graduate programme, which I joined. After three months they didn't know what to do with me, as it wasn't a particularly well-structured graduate programme like they are today.

After three months the owner said, 'Dane, I want you to be the general manager of this small company. About 100 people, and we are turning over about $3 million a year, but losing around $0.4 million a year. I want you to fix it'.

Clearly I did not know about how to be a CEO, having just finished my chemical engineering degree. But fortunately I had some experienced and supportive mentors who helped me learn and develop my leadership skills and competencies. One of those people would be in my leadership lifeline (described earlier).

One day at 6.00 am (I was always there when the factory opened), the owner arrives. I'm down on the factory floor and he comes in the back through one of the factory doors and he's looking around, so he yells out, 'Where's Dane?' I see him at the back so I call out, 'Here I am'. He comes across and says, 'Dane, I just want to congratulate you on doing a fantastic job'. And he writes me a cheque for $5000. (Now this was in 1984, so $5000 was a lot of money relative to my salary.) He then says, 'Keep up the great work'.

The next week he arrives again at my factory at 6.00 am. I see him coming and think, great, another bonus. I go across to him and he verbally tears me to shreds in front of the factory team members, and for what, I cannot remember. I walk away totally confused and demotivated.

This story illustrates the power of the leader's shadow. Leaders' words, actions and behaviours have a massive impact on their teams. It's paramount, therefore, that leaders show consistency. Giving me a bonus was incredible but then abusing me a few days later for no apparent reason completely confused me.

Let me further explain the concept of your leadership shadow; it is effectively your positional power. As a CEO your shadow is immense, as it is multiplicative. Your shadow comes through in your words, who you spend time with, how you react to news (good and bad), who you pay incentives to, who you promote, and even in your calendar. When you walk into the office, the team knows within five minutes whether you're in a good mood or a bad mood, or at least they will have an opinion. It might feel stressful at first for you because people are watching you constantly for signals, but over time you become used to the fact that your positional power has an immense impact on the business.

If you are still struggling to understand this, think about your parents and their impact on you. Or, if you are a parent, think about how your children copy you from a young age. Being a parent is a great example of the power of a leadership shadow and how people (you with your parents or your children) react because of your shadow.

To stay aware of your shadow and its impact requires discipline. To assist, find someone you trust on your team to be an observer. Ask them to quickly share with you if they see a negative impact from your interactions with the team.

Founder story

Roland was like so many founder CEOs and was always running at full speed with a wide range of challenges and issues popping up multiple times a day.

His problem was that his leadership shadow was one of conflict avoidance with his team — so decisions took too long to be made, or worse still, the team gave up coming to him with issues as they knew he would avoid the difficult conversation needed to resolve the issue.

In discussions with him, he honestly did not see himself like this. He thought instead that he was an inclusive and democratic leader. Once he understood the impact of his behaviours, he progressively increased his openness to engage in those tough conversations and in his decisiveness while also maintaining his bias for inclusivity.

Monday reflection

Are you honestly aware of your leadership shadow? On Monday, ask your co-founder or member of the leadership team to be an ongoing observer for you and provide real-time feedback if they feel your leadership shadow was neutral or negative.

The top nine impactful leadership responsibilities

Earlier in this chapter, I shared the disciplined leadership characteristics that impactful leaders exhibit in their leadership style. Now, I want to share the nine core responsibilities that founder CEOs must execute in order to scale and create substantial businesses, and turn their vision into reality.

Leadership **responsibilities** describe *what you do as the leader* — the deliberate, repeatable actions, initiatives and decisions that move the company forward. These are the core activities that enable achievement of your vision. If we created a job description for the CEO, most of these responsibilities would be listed as core competencies required for the role.

1. Build a sustainable business — a dynasty

I love the concept of a dynasty. Let me explain. I'm a sports nut, and in sport certain teams create legacies that last for decades. Think about English Premier League football — teams like Manchester City, Manchester United, Chelsea, Arsenal and Liverpool have built lasting dynasties. In Spanish football, it's Real Madrid and Barcelona. These teams don't win the championship every year but they are always in contention, year after year, decade after decade. They have built substantial fan bases and revenue because of this winning mentality, and record.

That's the type of business you want to build. Your company shouldn't have a few good years followed by a massive decline. You must design your business to thrive over the long haul and weathering inevitable challenges without a 'boom, splat' trajectory — where you experience two or three exceptional years followed by a massive revenue and profit miss. A sustainable business evolves, adapts and keeps growing its market share, revenue and cash flow.

The other benefit of great dynasties is that they are enviable brands that people want to join and stay with. Building a dynasty is a virtuous circle, attracting talent, delivering exceptional results, building the brand, growing revenue and profit, attracting talent, and so on.

It is easy to identify your vision of a business that delivers year after year, but this is difficult to achieve. In the next four chapters I will share the key elements that disciplined leaders execute to build businesses that become dynasties.

2. Great leaders paint the vision and communicate it (over and over again)

In Chapter 4 we will dive deeper into defining your company's vision, but for now let's assume you have one. One of your most important responsibilities as CEO is to build the strategy and the specific actions that will bring that vision to life, and then communicate it over and over and over again. There is a reason why I say the word 'over' three times in the previous sentence. Business success depends on the entire organisation understanding the company's direction and plans. This means repeating the vision and strategy over and over and over again.

One of my favourite analogies here is Taylor Swift performing *Shake It Off*. When she was in Singapore in 2024, a journalist asked her how many times she'd performed the song. Her response? 'Probably three million times — and I'd happily do it another three million'. And yet, if you saw her perform it live tonight, you'd feel as though she was singing it for the very first time, with full energy and enthusiasm.

As a CEO, you must deliver your vision and strategy with the same passion and energy — over and over and over again — until every single person in the company knows and supports it. Research shows that people need to hear a message, such as the company's vision and strategy seven or eight times before it sinks in, and they remember it.

Founder story

Lucy was a founder CEO of a business that started in 2017. Early on, as the team grew, she knew the benefit of all-hands meetings to ensure the team was aware of, and aligned with, the company's direction.

When COVID-19 arrived, the team needed to be reduced to survive as revenue declined significantly.

In 2023, although Lucy had rebuilt her team to over 100, she had not rebooted her communication. It had simply disappeared as a habit. We worked together to reboot and relaunch a strong communication platform, including monthly all-hands meetings, a CEO newsletter, skip-level lunches (refer to Chapter 3), and regular reach-outs from her to recognise key staff. This engagement was immensely powerful in aligning the team and the whole organisation behind what Lucy knew would take the business to the next level.

Monday reflection

Do you need to reboot your communication program post-COVID or kick-start one?

3. Disciplined leaders create committed teams

To ensure the best decisions are made you must assemble a strong team of people who complement your skills by speaking up and offering fresh perspectives, and confidently challenging you.

Beyond assembling a capable team, you also need to create an environment in which people feel valued, energised and committed to the company's success. There is extensive research confirming that employees who feel good about the company are far more likely to stay and contribute at a high level.

Earlier in the chapter, we covered leadership characteristics and number three was *Leaders need a clear purpose*. A great vision and powerful purpose only come to life with disciplined messaging. A compelling purpose, well-articulated over and over again (as per the Taylor Swift analogy), will make people feel good about the company and inspire them to move the company towards its vision.

4. Disciplined leaders allocate resources wisely

A very important responsibility of leaders is to allocate resources optimally, where resources are funds, people and time, while balancing the needs of all the stakeholders in the business.

When we talk about stakeholders, most people just think about employees, customers and shareholders. Your stakeholder ecosystem is much broader. It consists of:

- Leadership team
- Employee base
- Customers
- Suppliers and business partners
- Investors and banks
- Regulators (depending on your industry)
- Government
- Local community
- Your family
- You. It shouldn't be a surprise that you are one of the stakeholders and deserve to be considered in the allocation of resources.

Your job as a leader is to balance all these stakeholders, but without trying to please everyone. Balancing doesn't mean making everyone happy; it means ensuring that no critical stakeholder is ignored or blindsided.

5. Impactful leaders constantly drive change with urgency

As a founder CEO, the product or service you start with in year one is rarely the same as in year three. Disciplined leaders continuously consider their existing offering and whether it is optimum for the market today and in the future. They are considering how to refine or exit products, and how to move on to more attractive opportunities as the market evolves.

I've seen this time and time again with startups — the original concept they launched will often look dramatically different by the time they reach full scale. If you aren't constantly thinking about how to refine or disrupt your own business, a competitor will do it for you.

Similarly, you need to be constantly assessing your team members in terms of their performance and competency, and whether they are developing in line with what is required from them in the business. If not, then change will be required.

The founder CEO also sets the tempo for the company. There's a noticeable difference in energy when you are in the office versus when you're not. Your presence alone changes the dynamic. However, there are actions you can implement to increase the pace, such as back-to-back meetings on key initiatives, all-hands meetings, leadership team meetings and one-on-ones. More on how to hold these meetings to ensure urgency and focus can be found in Chapter 5.

Let me use President Trump as an example here. People may not agree with his strategies, decisions and how he does things, but you have to give him credit for driving change every minute of the day. He is constantly using every lever possible to push forward for what he believes is right for America.

Your job is to drive urgency, push the business forward, and instil a culture of continuous improvement. You, as the leader, should be pleased with progress but never fully satisfied — always striving for the next level of performance. Andy Pearson, the former head of global consulting firm McKinsey, and former Chairman of Yum! Brands, used to say, 'When you are ten per cent up, run the business like you are ten per cent down'. This ensures ongoing urgency for change and improvement.

6. Disciplined leaders measure the right things

Disciplined and impactful leaders have a unique ability to zoom in and out. They can operate at 10 000 feet — focusing on vision, strategy and big-picture priorities — but they also know when to drop into the details and fix something small before it becomes a big problem. A good example of how to do this is asking 'Why?', three times in three different ways, when you are investigating an issue with your team. When you are comfortable that the team has evaluated an issue or opportunity to the appropriate level of detail it is time to pop back up to 10 000 feet. If you are not happy, then keep pushing to understand, as this may surface a gap in their thinking.

An important lever is identifying the critical measures that truly represent the health and performance of your business. In the next chapter we will cover the importance of key performance indicators (KPIs) and how to use a balanced scorecard covering customer, operations, people and financial measures to accurately gauge your progress. Disciplined leaders definitely trust their instinct but are also maniacal in leveraging data and information to track the progress of the business. A Monday Ready question for you is, 'Are your business metrics right for your business in its current stage or should they be revised?'

The best leaders are agile, knowing when to dive deep and when to step back.

Founder story

Moh was a founder CEO who struggled with changing his thinking from strategic to detailed and then back to strategic. He would be 'stuck in the weeds' during crises, which happens a lot in a startup. He couldn't pull himself back up to a strategic level, which ultimately limited his effectiveness. He broke through this, initially by just becoming aware of this as an issue, and then we worked on approaches for him to reset. The three that worked best for him were:

- Schedule time each week for strategic reflection, specifically by asking himself whether he was prioritising his effort on the biggest opportunities (which he had previously identified) and whether the team was making progress against those plans.
- At the start of each week, he would challenge himself to ensure that his time/calendar is focused on building the company and not just on building the product.
- Identifying and tasking someone he trusted in the team to point out when he was stuck in the detail.

Monday reflection

How do you deliberately move from detail to strategic to detail to strategic again? Which of the above approaches could work for you, or do you have your own approach that works? Is there something you can do differently on Monday?

7. Disciplined leaders take responsibility and leverage recognition

When things go wrong, disciplined leaders don't look for excuses or scapegoats. Instead, they look in the mirror and ask themselves:

- What could I have done differently to prevent this issue?
- Were there warning signs I ignored?
- How can I adjust my leadership approach going forward to ensure this doesn't happen again?

A prime example of this is the banking industry. Large-scale fraud or corporate mismanagement, often involving issues the CEOs were completely unaware of, has resulted in the firing of many CEOs at major financial institutions over the years. As the leader they bear ultimate responsibility, whether they know about the issue or not. So, you need to take the initiative, ask difficult questions and carefully monitor progress.

On the flip side, when there is a win or success in part of the business, the credit should go to the team. A strong leader quickly recognises the individual and the team for the success, even if the leader played a key part. Recognition and appreciation go a long way in reinforcing positive behaviours and building a culture of trust and motivation. We'll explore this concept of building a recognition culture further in Chapter 4.

Monday reflection

How much recognition are you doing today? Can you double it, starting Monday?

8. Disciplined leaders *own* something

No matter how big the company gets, the CEO must remain personally involved in key areas of the business.

Early-stage founder CEOs are naturally hands-on, deeply involved in product development, customer relationships and hiring decisions.

As the company scales, their role shifts, but complete detachment could lead to a disconnection with what is really happening in the business. A CEO should always 'own' something critical, whether it's a major client relationship, a critical product innovation, a significant partnership opportunity or a development program for upcoming leaders.

This hands-on leadership ensures that you stay connected to the core of the business. It also signals to the team that you are here to help and are comfortable owning major projects.

9. Disciplined leaders know when to leave

Knowing when to exit — whether it's from a meeting, a dinner or even a leadership role — is an underrated but essential skill.

- **In meetings:** All meetings can get to the point of diminishing returns when it is clear that you do not have the information to make a decision, or the conversation starts going in circles with no new insights being generated. When this happens it's time to break. Sometimes your early exit signals that you have trust in the team to handle things without you.

- **At events:** Whether it's a networking dinner or a corporate function, lingering past your impact window can dilute your presence. My experience is that as the night progresses, and if people are drinking alcohol, someone will come up to you and say something they will regret in the morning. One of my catch phrases is, 'Nothing good happens after 9 o'clock'.

- **In your role:** This is the hardest decision of all. I've been a CEO five times, and each tenure lasted around five years. For me, five years has been right, giving me enough time to build a strong team and drive major change, and maintain my passion and interest. After five years I personally believe you need fresh energy and ideas. With that said, if you are a founder, growing a business from scratch to significant valuation in five years is difficult to achieve, so a longer period of time is likely required.

Staying beyond your effective period can be detrimental. Leaders who overstay often hold on to power rather than serving the company's best interests. Knowing when to step away is just as important as knowing when to step up.

In summary, below are the nine responsibilities of a disciplined and impactful leader:

1. Build a sustainable business — a dynasty.
2. Paint the vision and communicate it (over and over again).
3. Create committed teams.
4. Allocate resources.
5. Constantly drive change with urgency.
6. Measure the right things.
7. Take responsibility and leverage recognition.
8. Own something.
9. Know when to leave.

As with the earlier discussion on leadership characteristics, I suggest you review this list critically. First, do you agree with each responsibility? Is there something missing? Would you remove or adjust any of these? Once you've fine-tuned the list to a version that resonates most with you, then assess yourself against it. What are you especially good at? Where do you struggle? What are you not doing that you must do? Where do you need to build competency?

I recognise this is a long list, and realistically, you won't master all of these overnight.

Start by identifying the four or five areas where you naturally excel — those will become habits more quickly. Then, be mindful of the others and work on strengthening them through awareness and deliberate practice.

I encourage you to keep this list handy and reflect on it regularly — every week, every month, every quarter and every year. How are you progressing? Where do you need to improve? Implementing discipline around these responsibilities will require deliberate action.

Monday ready

Disciplined and impactful leadership does not just happen. It results from becoming a *relentless student* of leadership and *deliberately* investing in your leadership journey. It involves observing leaders in action, researching successful leaders, and reflecting on the opportunities that exist in fine-tuning your own leadership style. Knowing what outstanding leadership looks like positions you to authentically copy it.

This chapter also shared the concept of your leadership shadow, and the most impactful characteristics (*leadership style*) and responsibilities (*leadership actions*) that a leader must learn to execute to maximise their probability of creating a business that aligns with their vision.

There was a lot to absorb in this chapter, so the key takeaways are shared below.

Reflect on the key takeaways list. Focus on only two or three changes to be made this Monday and endeavour to repeat them frequently enough over the next month that they start to become habits. Be aware that your leadership evolution may require you doing 'less' of certain things, such as overreacting to bad news. Keep these opportunities in mind.

Next month, move on to another two or three changes and again, endeavour to demonstrate them frequently. And so on, each month, until you feel you have mastered this, or your own, list of leadership characteristics and responsibilities.

In the next chapter, I will show you why trust is so important in a business and how it is the foundation upon which you can then create accountability within your organisation.

Key takeaways

Translate your life journey into your leadership journey.

1. Become a student of leadership
2. Leadership characteristics:
   - Person of hope
   - Simplifier
   - Purpose-driven
   - Role model
   - Respectful
   - Empowering
   - Trusts their gut
   - Speaks last
   - Confident with humility
   - Relentless student
3. Leverage your leadership shadow
4. Leadership responsibilities:
   - Build a sustainable business — a dynasty.
   - Paint the vision and communicate it (over and over again).
   - Create committed teams.
   - Allocate resources.
   - Drive change with urgency.
   - Measure the right things.
   - Take responsibility and leverage recognition.
   - Own something.
   - Know when to leave.

CHAPTER 3

Build trust and accountability through disciplined behaviours

In this chapter, we focus on those deliberate leadership behaviours that build trust in your team and organisation, and lead to a culture of accountability. We introduce the six levers of trust and the five levers of accountability. To explain these concepts in more detail and the behaviours that you can implement to create trust and accountability, we will look at these three areas:

- How to determine the level of trust in your business. Leaders have a bias to focus on what they measure, so we need to assess trust levels.
- What are the six levers that disciplined leaders execute to build trust?
- What are the five levers that create a culture of accountability?

The connection between trust and accountability

A lazy view held by some leaders is that it is not possible to deliberately build a culture of trust and accountability in a business because these elements are so difficult to measure, and are equally challenging to target and influence. I have learned that the level of trust and accountability in a business is measurable, and it is possible to improve them if you are a disciplined leader.

Recall from the introduction that a disciplined leader knows that discipline beats vision: results are achieved when the leader is *deliberate* and *self-aware*, and consistently *role-models* the behaviours they expect from others, while evolving and reinventing their leadership as new challenges arise. Every decision is an intentional choice — the leader models the right behaviours and their every action predictably moves the team and the company closer to its vision.

Trust is the foundation on which successful teams work together, because belief in each other and a desire to support one another lead to individual accountability. Essentially, your goal as the leader is to create an environment in which individuals do not want to let you or their colleagues down.

With trust also comes psychological safety. Psychological safety refers to a shared belief within a team or organisation that it is safe to take interpersonal risks, such as speaking up without concern about being judged or criticised. The benefits of psychological safety include honest debate, tolerance for mistakes, and the confidence to speak up. This fosters lower staff turnover and a more productive working environment. Not surprisingly, your own demonstration of trust has a massive impact on the team. Recall the *leadership shadow* concept from Chapter 2 — your behaviours are multiplicative. If you show trust, your team will as well.

Now you might think trust is a soft, intangible skill and therefore not a business priority. However, there is considerable research to confirm the impact of trust on your business, including a Slack 2023 Global Survey of more than 10 000 employees. It found that those who felt trusted by their manager were twice as productive, more than twice as focused, and 4.3 times more satisfied in their jobs.

Many of my clients tell me their team is not accountable, and they often believe it's the team's fault. They are unsure how they can change their team's behaviour. Having a great vision for the company and its culture will not build accountability — only disciplined behaviours from you will achieve that.

Trust is the foundation for teams to work together. When there is a mutual belief in and support for one another, individuals are far more likely to hold themselves accountable. A useful analogy is sports. Elite teams trust that each person on the team will execute their role. A football player doesn't always need to cover someone else's tackle because they trust their better-positioned teammate will make it. Your team operates the same way; to operate optimally they need to believe that other team members will do their jobs well. Your team may not stay with you if there is limited trust. Even if they stay, they won't hit their goals unless there is individual accountability across the whole team.

Measuring trust in your business

Many leaders struggle with how to measure an abstract concept like trust. However, it is possible to measure if you break trust down into behaviours in different situations where individuals and teams interact and rely on each other. The absolute score in this survey is not important; it is instead about identifying issues that can be resolved. By resolving issues, the level of trust will improve.

The below template is one you can use to survey your team and evaluate the level of trust. You may think that your team will not be honest in their feedback. To ensure they are, you must make sure their responses are confidential. Remember: this survey is not about getting a score. It's about pinpointing what might be undermining trust in your organisation and so help you to see how and where trust can be built.

Conducting the trust survey

The following ten questions in table 3.1 (overleaf) are used to assess trust in your business. Distribute them to your team and ask for either a Yes/No response or a score out of five, where:

5 = Happens all the time

3 = Occasionally happen

1 = Never happens

To encourage clearer responses, you may decide to veto neutral scores (3s) and require employees to commit to either a 2 or a 4 if they are considering a 3. As mentioned above, ensure the collection process is confidential as this increases the probability that the survey participants will be honest.

Table 3.1 Sample trust survey of the characteristics of teams with high levels of trust

On a scale of 1 (low) to 5 (high), rank our team on the following behaviours		
	Trust survey question	**Examples of behaviours that would rate a 5**
1	Is there always clear respect for each other in team meetings?	In meetings, team members listen and speak respectfully to each other, even during heated or challenging discussions.
2	Is there always clear respect for each other outside of team meetings?	Outside of meetings, team members listen and speak respectfully to each other, even during heated or challenging discussions. People do not criticise each other outside of meetings.
3	Do all members of the team speak up with their honest views, even on controversial topics?	People always speak up honestly on all topics, and even on topics where there may be significant disagreement and some emotion.
4	Is the team honest about what is happening in the business?	The team members are open and honest in their assessment of the business performance: what's working and what's not, and in identifying issues in the business.
5	Is there transparency and sharing of information across the team?	The team members openly share information; even if it may not be as positive as they would like, and may affect how the team sees their performance.

6	When conflicts arise, do team members resolve them rather than escalating issues to the CEO?	The team works together to resolve their own issues, disagreements and conflicts, as opposed to turning to the founder CEO to arbitrate.
7	When a commitment is at risk of being missed, does the team work together to support one another rather than assigning blame?	The team works together to resolve issues and deliver commitments, as opposed to criticising each other for missed deliverables.
8	Are there no factions or hierarchies in the group (e.g. Team A vs Team B)?	The team considers each member to be an equal participant and judges all views equally, irrespective of the contributor.
9	Is there loyalty and a firm belief in each other, even during challenges?	The team members believe in each person's ability to deliver against goals.
10	Is there psychological safety within the team?	Each member of the team feels comfortable about speaking up and not feeling judged or open to personal criticism.

Analysing and acting on the results

Rather than calculating an average score, look at the frequency distribution of scores. Identify trends and where there are clusters of ratings. This highlights the key areas that need improvement. At your next leadership team meeting, discuss these results. Do not attempt to determine who gave which score. Instead, work with your team to identify behaviours that are undermining trust and determine specific actions to improve them.

Figure 3.1 (overleaf) is an example of a completed survey that illustrates how a completed survey could look, with the frequency distribution highlighting opportunity areas marked by (x), and positive areas marked by (✓).

Characteristics of teams with high levels of trust

	On a scale of 1 (low) to 5 (high), rank our team on the following behaviours:	1	2	3	4	5
✓	Is there always clear respect for each other in team meetings?	1	/ 2	// 3	/// 4	// 5
✓	Is there always clear respect for each other outside of team meetings?	1	/ 2	// 3	/// 4	// 5
x	Do all members of the team speak up with their honest views, even on controversial topics?	1	//// 2	/// 3	/ 4	5
	Is the team honest about what is happening in the business?	1	2	///// 3	/// 4	5
	Is there transparency and sharing of information across the team?	1	/ 2	//// 3	// 4	/ 5
	When conflicts arise, do team members resolve them rather than escalating issues to the CEO?	1	/ 2	/// 3	/// 4	/ 5
x	When a commitment is at risk of being missed, does the team work together to support one another rather than assigning blame?	1	//// 2	/// 3	/ 4	5
✓	Are there no factions or hierarchies in the group (e.g., Team A vs. Team B)?	1	2	/ 3	//// 4	/// 5
	Is there loyalty and a firm belief in each other, even during challenges?	1	/ 2	//// 3	/// 4	5
x	Is there psychological safety within the team?	/ 1	// 2	// 3	// 4	/ 5

Figure 3.1 Example of a completed survey

Figure 3.1 shows the power of having a frequency distribution, and also illustrates why I suggested vetoing 3s — because being neutral, it tends to get the most votes. The most positive areas were questions 1, 2 and 8 — *respect for each other* and *no factions*. The most negative, with the highest number of 1s, 2s and 3s, were questions 3, 7 and 10 — *team members not speaking up, supporting one another to hit commitments, and psychological safety.* This prioritisation enables the team to focus their discussion on potential improvements.

You may think this would be difficult to do with your team because they will not be honest when completing the form. To resolve this, you must ensure there is confidentiality in the approach. You can achieve this by setting the survey up in SurveyMonkey, or have an assistant collect hard copies in blank envelopes, or even by using a facilitator, such as myself, to gather the feedback. I've done this many times with clients and rarely have I found that people have not been honest when the surveys were confidential.

The six levers to build trust

Building trust in your team and the organisation is the foundation for creating a sustainable and successful business. The two key reasons for this are that people will stay with you longer, and they'll have a high level of accountability as they want to deliver for you and their team.

However, this is where founder CEOs often, not surprisingly, struggle. When the business is a small startup, the team members are likely to be predominantly good friends with similar backgrounds, perhaps having met at university where they were all doing the same or similar degrees. As the organisation grows to 20, 50 and more than 100 people, different skills are required in the business and the diversity of the team grows exponentially, beyond say the six engineers who started the company. The founder CEO must learn how to connect and lead this diverse group, which is a totally different skill than product creation, which was the initial focus of the company.

To assist these leaders, I have identified the six levers to build trust. They are easy for you to execute, and the more you practise them, the quicker they will become authentic habits. In a nutshell, it's like Newton's Third Law of Motion: *For every action, there is an equal and opposite reaction.* When you consistently execute the disciplined leadership actions to build trust and accountability, you can guarantee your team will mirror them back.

1. Role-model the right behaviours

It cannot be stated often enough: *role modelling is one of the most important elements of being a disciplined leader.* You need to constantly demonstrate the behaviours you expect from the team. Social learning theory, as developed by psychologist Albert Bandura, supports this. His research found that people emulate the behaviours they observe, particularly from those they respect. When leaders frequently show consistency between their words and actions, and these align with the company's values, it reinforces trust.

Founder story

Sam is a founder CEO who was frustrated by the lack of trust within his team. He runs a software startup that is expanding into Southeast Asia, but growth had slowed and collaboration within and across markets was non-existent. When I asked him what he thought the problem was, he said, 'The team members don't share information as they compete for sales and commissions. I don't feel they fully trust each other'.

We explored how the commission structure and his own behaviours might be shaping this environment. Sam admitted he had set up a bonus system to individually incentivise salespeople, with no team element, and he encouraged this 'lone wolf' approach in meetings as he thought this competitive rivalry would drive sales.

Once Sam recognised this, he realised that the first thing he needed to do was change the incentive system so it would have a large

---

team component to encourage collaboration. Secondly, he needed to role-model the behaviours of sharing information — leveraging best practice by encouraging multiple salespeople to work on deals together. And finally, he needed to recognise the team's performance as much, if not more, than recognition of individuals.

Over time, the salespeople responded in kind, creating a stronger culture of trust and sharing ideas that gave the business new momentum.

Monday reflection

Are you encouraging and recognising team-based performance to inspire trust and collaboration?

Role modelling behaviours — such as showing an authentic interest in people, being a skilled listener, showing strong personal control even in times of crisis, and stepping forward and taking responsibility in difficult times — all set examples of what you would also appreciate seeing in your team. When the team sees you role-model these behaviours they will copy you.

With that said, we are all human and will occasionally make mistakes due to the pressure of the role, or an error in judgement. When these situations arise, right the wrong quickly and be comfortable in acknowledging your mistake. You will remember that in Chapter 2 we discussed leadership characteristics where we identified that leaders must show humility and, at times, vulnerability. These moments of honesty can actually be the most powerful in building trust with your team. If you are open to admitting mistakes, it is more likely that your team will mirror you and be more comfortable in admitting their errors.

2. Build strong emotional intelligence

Many founder CEOs believe emotional intelligence (EI) is nothing more than the ability to read others. However, in his book *Emotional Intelligence: Why It Can Matter More Than IQ*, Daniel Goleman, one of the world experts in EI, defines it as having four critical components:

- **Self-awareness.** The ability to recognise and understand your emotions, strengths and limitations. Self-aware leaders are grounded and authentic, fostering trust by consistently showing up as their true selves. If you lack self-awareness, your team will see through inconsistencies, making it harder to build trust.
- **Self-management.** The ability to regulate emotions, stay calm under pressure, and respond thoughtfully rather than react impulsively. Leaders who manage their emotions will create stability, especially in high-stakes situations. A CEO who loses control or shifts moods unpredictably creates uncertainty, eroding the team's trust.
- **Social awareness.** The ability to recognise emotions in others, understand team dynamics, and sense the organisation's pulse. This is where empathy plays a key role. A CEO who is socially aware picks up on concerns before they escalate and can make people feel heard, which builds confidence and psychological safety, and trust.
- **Social skills.** This one is often not considered a priority by leaders. However, leaders who develop strong social skills and connect with their teams will significantly increase the level of trust the team has in them. To be clear, I am not suggesting you are trying to create new best friends in your business; this is about building a connection with the team beyond KPI discussions. The simplest lever to demonstrate your social skills is to use people's names, as people love to hear their name said by the CEO.

Each one in the above list is equally important. A founder CEO with strong EI builds trust because they:

- **demonstrate consistency** through self-awareness and self-management
- **make people feel valued** by connecting with the team, recognising emotions and responding appropriately
- **foster transparency** through clear and empathetic communication.

Some people feel that emotional intelligence is a quality that is inherent and can't be learned. However, like most leadership skills, it *is* learnable if you apply yourself and use the above framework to guide you. This is another example of one of the elements of being a disciplined leader; that is, being a *relentless student* and continuously investing in your personal learning and growth, adding new skills and competencies. Leaders who master emotional intelligence will create a workplace in which people feel safe, motivated and engaged, which is essential for building high-performance teams.

Let me tell you a story where one of my bosses failed in the above area and lost a significant amount of my trust.

A number of years ago my father had cancer and was on his journey to pass away. At the same time, there was a meeting that my boss wanted me to attend overseas. I knew my father only had a few weeks to live. However, my boss still said he required me at the meeting.

On the morning of the first day of the meeting, my mother called and gave me a sad update on my father's health. My father's condition distracted me during the morning meeting, limiting my participation in discussions. At the lunchbreak, my boss came up to me and addressed me quite aggressively, saying, 'Dane, I need you to participate. You're a key leader in this business. I need you to speak up'.

He knew I did not want to be at the meeting as he knew my father was passing away. With that said, he didn't show any empathy. Because of the way he spoke to me, I lost respect and trust in that leader.

This is an example of poor emotional intelligence. If a team member is not performing to their normal high standard, don't attack. Investigate why, as there may be a good reason.

To be clear, this does not mean you should accept ongoing poor performance if a team member is having personal issues. Investigate and identify how to support them, or move them to the side until they can contribute to their normal high standard.

3. Share information

Sam Walton, the founder of Walmart, famously said, 'The more you share, the more they care'. Leaders must provide the information for employees to do their jobs. Many leaders restrict information because of confidentiality concerns. In fact, the opposite is true — the more transparent you are, the greater the empowerment and trust within the team. Also, many leaders become caught up in the day-to-day running of the business and the crises that arise, often cancelling opportunities where they could share information with the broader team.

There are many ways to share information, such as via updates circulated over your digital platform; in all-hands meetings where you can provide it face-to-face; or by holding small gatherings with functional or operations teams. In Chapter 6 I will share the optimum approach and agenda to holding all-hands meetings.

The final idea is the simplest of all but often the least used. Just walking around the office chatting with team members is immensely powerful in communicating and connecting with the team.

Beyond business updates, the team and organisation need the information to perform their roles. I often see leaders restrict sharing of key financial or customer information because they are concerned about confidentiality and fear that someone may leave the company to join a competitor. My response to this is that people are more likely to leave if you *don't* provide the information. Sharing information is a critical way to build trust. When employees understand the broader picture, they feel more empowered and invested in the company's success. Sharing information also shows that you trust them, which leads to reciprocation, with them increasing their trust in you.

Monday reflection

How can you increase information sharing in the business to improve trust and ownership?

4. Interact frequently with leaders and the organisation

There are many ways to *deliberately* build strong connections — one-on-one meetings, team meetings, all-hands meetings and retreats.

Even though you may feel your company is still small, trust-building and strategy retreats are a powerful way to build deep relationships with your leadership team and broader groups of leaders, while also aligning the team on strategic priorities and key initiatives.

In table 3.2 is a two-day offsite agenda that have I facilitated for over 30 of my clients, some with organisations of fewer than 20 people. I have performed this task twice yearly for the past four years for one of my clients.

Table 3.2 Example of a two-day offsite agenda

Day 1	
Agenda item	**Rationale/Descriptor**
Setting the scene	CEO to update the team on the business and the objective for the offsite.
Multi-year goals	Finance leader shares the goals for the next three years.
Building trust session	Icebreakers used to increase the team's understanding of each other and increase trust and respect. Tools such as the Myers–Briggs Type Indicator (MBTI) or DiSC® can be powerful.

(continued)

Table 3.2 (continued)

Agenda item	Rationale/Descriptor
Values workshop	This is a session to validate the company's values, and includes actions for the leadership team to embed.
Day 2	
Strategy workshop	With the leadership group, identify the key strategic priorities and initiatives for the business to achieve the Multi-year goal.
Divisional/ functional plans	Divisions and functions to identify their initiatives.
Top talent review	Identify future leaders in the business and what development they need.
Wrap-up	CEO to close the retreat, identifying next steps for each leader.

Monday reflection

Is it time for an offsite to build trust and align the team around the strategies to achieve your vision?

Skip-level lunches

As a CEO, one of my favourite approaches for connecting with the team is what are called 'skip-level lunches'. These involve the CEO meeting directly with employees who are two or three levels down in the organisation.

Note that in the introduction I mentioned that some suggestions in the book may not be appropriate to implement given the size of your business, and skip-level lunches may be one of those you put off — for now.

In table 3.3 I lay out the rationale for these sessions, and the structured approach for conducting them.

Table 3.3 Skip-level lunches rationale and approach

Why are skip-level lunches impactful?	Logistics
• Enable you to communicate your company's strategy and vision clearly to the team that is closer to, or on, the front line. • Allow you to get feedback on the culture and the business — and so help you to stay in touch. • Reinforce the positive elements of your leadership shadow. • Research shows that of the 50 most valuable roles in a typical corporation, only 10 per cent report directly to a CEO; 60 per cent exist at the next level down; and 20 per cent are at the level below that. Therefore, it is critical for you to identify them and know them.	• Ask your assistant to schedule this every 4 weeks, or when you visit a location/division away from headquarters. • Invite a diverse range of people, covering tenure, level in the organisation, and division or function. Ensure you have a good percentage of operators or customer-facing staff. They do not need to be one level below your leadership team. They could be two, three or four down. Target 10 to 12 people. • Do not invite your direct reports — in fact, veto them!

The skip-level lunch meeting agenda

- Welcome the group and ask everyone to introduce themselves.
- Talk about your background (so they feel they know you better), then spend 15 minutes on the company's vision and strategy (*recall the Taylor Swift Shake It Off analogy in Chapter 1*). The team needs to see that you have clarity and passion around where you are taking the business.
- Push for Q&A on the strategy, as this helps to embed it. If it helps, plant some questions to get it going.

- Ask the following questions:
  - What do you like about the company?
  - What have you achieved in the last 3 months that you are particularly proud of?
  - What is working better now than 6 months ago?
  - What is not working or could work better?
  - What do you think I should know that I don't?
  - What would you do if you were in my position as CEO?

The above is an extremely powerful approach to build trust in the organisation. The first time you do this, it will feel like a bit of a clunky meeting, but over time it will feel more natural. I can assure you that regardless of how you feel, the team will love these meetings and tell the rest of the organisation how good it was. You will also learn things that are not working that you did not know about!

Disciplined leaders are deliberate in arranging the above at least once a month. Articulating the company's vision is a part of the approach, but only a small part. The majority of the approach is about understanding what is really happening in the business, and building a connection with people beyond your leadership team.

There is, however, one downside from these sessions! You will get a list of what is not working which you will need to address. By doing this you build trust; if you don't fix the issues, unfortunately, you erode trust!

5. Use trust-building tools

Psychometric testing is an excellent way to assess and understand team dynamics. Tools like Myers–Briggs, Clifton Strengths Finder, DiSC, Hogan, and scenario-based judgement tests provide valuable insights into individuals' strengths and their working styles. Sharing these results fosters greater understanding and collaboration among team members. As mentioned above, and shown in my example of a retreat agenda, these are useful exercises at offsites and retreats.

Founder story

James had a team of around 150 and they were spread out across Southeast Asia. This increased the complexity of building team camaraderie, a consistent company culture, alignment around strategy, and best practice sharing.

To offset this challenge, at least twice a year he brought the top 25 leaders together into one location for a two-day working session. Every time he did this he used a facilitator to perform a different psychometric test. Over the years, he probably covered eight of these tests. It is not that he was passionate about any of these being better than the others, it was simply a tool to inspire reflection and connection with each of his leaders.

The team valued the insights the tests provided to them, and they felt they were better leaders as a consequence.

Monday reflection

How can you use leadership or psychometric evaluations to help build trust and improve collaboration in your team?

A very simple approach to trust-building is through the use of icebreakers at the start of your leadership team meetings or social events, such as Friday drinks or dinners. Below I have included a few icebreaker questions you might find useful:

- A principle I lead my life by is ...
- Three core values that guide me at home and work are ...
- My friends would use the following three adjectives to describe me ...
- Tell us something about your childhood that would surprise this group ...

- Tell me about a person, whom you don't know but who has inspired you ...
- For as long as I can remember, I wanted to ...
- My superpower is ...

6. Be adept and proactive in handling conflict

You must be good at handling conflict, as it happens multiple times every day, if not every hour. Essential behaviours to better manage conflict include:

- **Recognise that confrontation is inevitable.** Avoiding it and thinking the situation will get better rarely works. You must be *deliberate* in identifying the conflict and addressing it.
- **Stay calm and unemotional.** This is tough to do, particularly if you are feeling personally connected to the issue. With that said, over time and with practice you can get better.
- **Focus on the problem, not the individual.** Do not allow your points to become personal, even if the other parties do.
- **Find common ground and solutions.** Coming to a comprehensive solution may require agreement over hundreds of points. Remain patient and work through it, issue by issue. Focus on the easier points first to generate some common ground and positive momentum that can be built upon.
- **Know when to walk away.** Sometimes, in conflict and during difficult discussions when you see that agreement is not possible, your most powerful action is to walk away. Similarly, choose whether it is worth your time to engage in a dispute or a point of difference; remember to 'choose your battles'.
- **'Eat the frog early'.** I love this expression. Strange as it may sound, this means tackling your most difficult task first thing in the morning. Putting it off won't make it easier — it will only weigh on your mind and distract you throughout the day. I have often said that I have never received a good news phone call

after 6 pm. This is because people call you first thing with good news, or immediately they receive it. However, most people, and customers for that matter, procrastinate and give you bad news at the end of the day or week.

- **Document it.** At the end of a confrontation or negotiation, documentation is critical. I've had many instances where I thought we agreed to an outcome during a discussion, only to realise later that the other person understood it differently. Before you leave a hard conversation, be sure to summarise and document what you have agreed upon. This ensures there is no ambiguity and no issues down the track.

The opening statement in any confrontation is crucial to a successful resolution. If you start with, 'I can't believe you did this!', the conversation is doomed before it begins. Instead, consider these alternatives:

- 'I value your perspective, and would appreciate hearing your reasoning behind your approach in situation X'.
- 'We may have different perceptions about X, so I'd like to understand your thinking before I share mine'.
- 'I'd like to discuss X. I believe we may have different ideas about how to approach Y, so I'd love to hear your perspective first'.

Developing your own introductory statements can significantly improve the tone and quality of your discussions.

A final suggestion for becoming more comfortable with conflict is simply to practise it. For the past 30 years, I've made it a habit to *always* ask for a discount when shopping, or an upgrade when checking into a hotel or flight. In effect, I'm practising conflict in low-stakes situations. The more you practise, the more natural it feels. My wife knows this routine well. When we check into a hotel, she won't unpack until I've gone back downstairs to ask for an upgrade. I'm always respectful, and I accept the answer without fuss. By the way, I succeed at least 25 per cent of the time!

Monday reflection

How can you practise handling conflict in your daily life? Could asking for a discount or an upgrade be a safe way to build confidence, while reaping some unexpected rewards?

Where do leaders struggle most with the six levers of trust?

The number one trust-building lever, and a defining trait of a disciplined leader, is role modelling. This is also the area where I see most leaders struggle. My recommendations are:

- Put 15 minutes into your calendar at the end of each week, or on the weekend, to reflect on how well you executed the six levers of trust, particularly role modelling. Target which areas you will work on, *starting Monday.*
- Appoint someone on your team to help guide you. It could be your chief of staff, head of HR, COO, or another trusted colleague who observes you in action and can offer direct, honest feedback. Be open to their input and identify what you will do differently *on Monday.*

Another common challenge to executing these initiatives stems from your scarcest resource: *time*. It may feel counterintuitive, but when your time is limited and everyone is competing for it, even the smallest signals can have the biggest impact on building trust. This is why *self-awareness* is one of a disciplined leader's most powerful tools. A short four- or five-word message to someone can mean a lot, precisely because they know how busy you are. Even when you are time-poor, you can still connect, signal presence, and build trust with your team.

Achieving your inspirational vision will only occur if you are *deliberate* in your approach to building trust and, consequently, accountability.

The five levers of accountability

Once trust is established, it sets the foundation for accountability. Accountability, and the team delivering upon their commitments, is the discipline required to make your vision a reality.

When people believe in one another and feel supported, they are far more likely to take ownership of their commitments and deliver on them. Your goal as a leader is to create an environment in which individuals feel trusted and are therefore motivated to meet expectations — an environment in which they don't want to let you, their peers or the business down.

This is where the five levers of accountability come into play. As we have seen, your *deliberate* actions build trust. Now, in this section we will see how your *deliberate* actions create a culture of accountability.

Let me first share a personal story about my own failure in accountability.

I once worked for a boss — let's call him Bob. Bob was a 'jiggler'; he constantly bounced his right foot up and down, especially when frustrated or angry. And he got angry a lot.

I was the CFO and had many non-finance responsibilities, including supply chain. One day we received an inquiry from a regulatory body and I asked my head of supply chain to draft a response. When I read the response I thought, 'This isn't great'. But life was busy — my wife and I had just welcomed our third child home — so I let it slide. I told my head of supply chain to send it in to the regulatory body, which he did while also copying in Bob.

A few days later, on my one day of paternity leave, my phone rang at 8:00 am.

It was Bob.

I could hear his foot bouncing as he asked, 'Dane, did you see that submission?'

'Yes, Bob, I did'.

'Were you happy with it?'

'No, Bob, I wasn't'.

He exploded. Yelling, swearing, calling me lazy. 'Dane, you want to be a f…g CEO. You'll never be a f…g CEO if you show this lack of accountability, and acceptance of poor-quality work'.

For 15 minutes he yelled at me. By the end I was nearly in tears. As he calmed down, he said, 'I want you to remember this conversation'.

I replied, 'Bob, I'll tell my grandchildren about it but without the swear words. Thank you'.

On Monday morning I walked into his office, closed the door and said, 'Bob, thank you for the call. You were right. I didn't show accountability, and the quality of that work was unacceptable. I let the business down and have learned from this. But Bob, if you ever speak to me like that again, I won't come to work the next day. Thank you'.

And I walked out.

The lesson? Bob was right. I was not deliberately accountable for my team's work; I accepted work that wasn't the right quality, and it put our business at risk.

This is the number one lever to build accountability in the organisation. You, as a disciplined leader, must be a role model of accountability. This is the first building block to create the culture of accountability.

Let me now share the five levers of accountability.

1. Be a role model of accountability

Many founder CEOs find this especially difficult because their roles often feel like controlled chaos. One moment they're deep in product development, the next they're in a critical customer meeting, troubleshooting engineering issues, or supporting a young and inexperienced team. If this sounds familiar, you're not alone. It's the reality for most leaders as they scale.

I have identified a few initiatives that can build the disciplined habits that bring focus and consistency to meeting your commitments. Simply put, accountability is *doing what you say you will do when you say you will do it.*

Here are some ideas to assist if this is an area in which you struggle:

- **Put your tasks in the calendar with their deadlines.** Use your calendar to remind yourself of outputs you have promised; copy in the person you have promised them to as well.
- **Put time in your calendar to do the work required to deliver your commitment.** Many leaders do this but the slot is often taken by more urgent tasks which may not be as important as your commitment. This is an ongoing balance to achieve, but endeavour to hold firm, as your role modelling of accountability is critical to achieve a culture of accountability.
- **Ask a team member to follow you up on your commitments.** It could be your assistant or a chief of staff.
- **Show discipline in meetings.** Start on time, set clear agendas, be present in the meetings and not distracted by your phone or email, and finish the meeting on time. This may seem insignificant to you, but this disciplined approach to meetings sets a tone for the organisation. Remember leadership shadow in Chapter 2; the team is watching and will copy you. If you show discipline in your meetings, they will as well. More on how to manage your meetings is in Chapter 5.

Founder story

Paul was initially my most frustrating client. He cancelled our meetings with limited notice, or when we did go ahead, he was always at least 15 minutes late.

Not surprising to me was that his organisation was similarly chaotic and struggled to hit any of its targets.

(continued)

Our immediate focus was creating discipline around his meetings — holding firm to start and finish times. If a meeting needed more time, an additional meeting was scheduled rather than running over. He employed an assistant to manage him to his schedule. This included messaging him, warning that a meeting needed to be finished in 5 minutes, or at times, stepping into a meeting and encouraging Paul to come to his next meeting or call.

The meeting discipline was step one, and gradually he rolled out the other levers of accountability.

Creating meeting discipline was a surprisingly powerful accountability lever within Paul's organisation.

Monday reflection

Is there discipline in your meeting approach? If not, then make a change on Monday.

2. Make clear the deliverables expected from your team and follow up relentlessly

The critical element of Lever 2 is to invest the time in explaining exactly what you need to accomplish, specifically the high-level goals and deadlines. One way to think about this is to deconstruct your vision, identifying the three or four outcomes that will contribute to the achievement of your vision. These targeted outcomes do not need to be a long period out; they could actually be what you need to achieve this month and quarter.

Next, cascade targets down from a broad company level to a divisional, functional or team level, and finally to an individual level. It is this discipline in setting targets and initiatives that will move you towards your vision.

Consider using a balanced scorecard. What I mean by a balanced scorecard is that you have a broad range of targets: financial, customer, functional and operating. Refer to table 3.4 for an example of a balanced scorecard. This is more detailed than you may need today in your business but the concept of having targets across all these areas is valid for businesses of any size.

Table 3.4 **Example of a balanced scorecard**

Safety, compliance and diversity	Operations
• LTIFR (lost time injury frequency rate) • Compliant with labour laws • Inclusion and diversity targets	• Productivity measurements (e.g. output/FTE) • Quality measurements • Up time on your digital platform • Cost of goods measures or performance vs standard costs
Customer	**Financial (vs last year and vs budget)**
• Key accounts: _% of revenue • Customer segments: _% of revenue • cNPS +50; +95% customer retention	• Organic growth: +% • New business revenue % • Annual recurring revenue $ • Gross margin % • Above unit costs or General & admin costs in $ and as a % of sales • EBIT + % • Free cash flow $_ • Debtor days < 60 days
People: 'Employer of Choice'	
• No leadership team (LT) vacancies • Succession plans in place with 80% of roles filled internally and 2 internal successors for all LT roles • Performance development plans developed for LT & LT-1 • eNPS +50 • Staff turnover < 10%	

Monday reflection

Could you identify and build a balanced scorecard for your business?

When you're setting targets, think in terms of inputs and outcomes (these are sometimes referred to as 'lead vs lag' indicators). For example, for sales targets, inputs could be the number of cold calls made per week, the number of client meetings, and the number of proposals made per week or per month. The outputs or outcomes are your win rate percentage, deal size and your new revenue.

Consider phasing of your targets as well. What's your monthly target? Is there a quarterly target? Is there a half-year target? The timing of your targets will affect the team's focus, so be thoughtful about what targets you may want your team to focus on this month, this quarter, or the first or second half of the year.

The second component of Accountability Lever 2 is to follow up. I love the quote attributed to former US president, Ronald Reagan. He was with the then president of the Soviet Union, Mikhail Gorbachev, and they were negotiating disarmament. The quote he used was, in effect, 'I trust you, but I need to verify'. This is one of my favourite quotes that I use when I'm mentoring founder CEOs. Just because you want verification or validation that someone has delivered against a goal, doesn't mean you don't trust them.

Accounting firms are great examples. Accounting firms make billions of dollars each year simply verifying what management says they have done. You need to do the same with your team as a founder CEO. I trust you, but I need to verify that something's been done and to the right level of quality.

In terms of verification, the following are useful approaches:

- **First informal follow-up.** Frequent, informal catch-ups are powerful. It could be at the coffee machine. It might be sending someone a message while you're on a Zoom call. I have found that it is crucial for your team to know you are aware of and are tracking their progress against targets.

- **Formal sessions.** These are also extremely powerful — and the frequency of your meetings drives urgency. For example, if you have a major tender due in two weeks' time, you should not wait until the day before to review that tender. You should set up short formal meetings beforehand to ensure the team is on track. *Trust, but verify.* So, continuing with the example: today is Monday and the proposal is due next Friday, in 12 days' time. I would want to meet with my team on Wednesday this week, Friday of this week, Tuesday of next week, and then maybe Thursday morning before the proposal is due on the Friday. Now these meetings could be just ten minutes or an hour or two. This is you checking on the progress, that the quality of the tender is to the standard you want or, in a longer meeting, diving deeper to provide your insights. *Remember Bob the jiggler*; I should have done all of the above, and I didn't.

- One-on-one meetings are effective with KPI follow-up; there will be more on this in Chapter 5. Consider using a template. See the example in table 3.5 (overleaf) of a template I use regularly with my teams. This template could be in Google Docs or something similar, and shows the team updating progress continuously against an initiative for all to see.

- **Monday check-ins.** Another follow-up approach is the Monday morning check-in where you have all your direct reports attend for a maximum of 30 minutes. Each person then shares the three things they are working on this week that you should know about, and whether they need your help or that of any of their peers.

Table 3.5 Example objectives tracking template

Individual	30-day objective and tasks (status included in brackets)	3-month objective and tasks (status included in brackets)
1. (name)_____	Objective: _____ Tasks to accomplish (and status):	Objective: _____ Tasks to accomplish (and status):
2. (name)_____	Objective: _____ Tasks to accomplish (and status):	Objective: _____ Tasks to accomplish (and status):
3. (name)_____	Objective: _____ Tasks to accomplish (and status):	Objective: _____ Tasks to accomplish (and status):

You may be thinking the above sounds like micromanagement. It is not. This is particularly important to do in the scaling phase of the business, as new people are coming onboard and you're embedding a culture of accountability. Over time, with greater trust in your team, and in their teams, you may reduce your follow-up. However, I would caution you on this. Remember, 'Trust but verify' is a critical leadership discipline that moves the business towards your vision.

Monday reflection

Are you doing enough 'trusting but verifying' in your business? What can you do differently on Monday?

3. Ensure visibility of targets and the individual's/team's performance

Research shows that people respond to visible targets and leaderboards. Each member of your sales team, without exception, wants to be the top of the sales leaderboard, and no-one wants to be at the bottom.

Sharing information, such as on leaderboards, is a powerful way to drive ownership and accountability for performance. Think about sports competitions. All the teams want to be at the top of the leaderboard, not the bottom. More on this later.

Another example of this is in factory or industrial environments where there is a safety board that tracks many measures, including the number of days since a lost time injury (LTI). The team is always immensely proud of building up that number, and is inspired to stay aware and careful.

Another way of creating visibility is to have what I would refer to as *stewardship meetings*, where individuals or teams present their monthly or quarterly performance to a broader group, including their peers. In this way people can see who's doing well and who they can learn from. It also creates a pressure on those people who aren't doing as well. Recognition awards are yet another powerful way of creating visibility over performance. I'll talk more about recognition and building a deliberate culture in Chapter 4.

Monday reflection

What scoreboard can you share or create to drive performance in the business?

4. Delegate with ownership

Delegation is the next lever to create accountability. Why is delegation so important in creating a culture of accountability? There are two key reasons:

- It gives you time to focus on other areas — where you could have an even greater impact than with the responsibility you delegated.
- Delegation is a way to empower someone and provide them with an opportunity to grow or show their capability.

However, there are lots of reasons leaders don't delegate:

- You don't want a loss of control.
- You are a perfectionist and fear messing up.
- You don't want to invest the time to explain the task.
- Prior unsatisfactory experiences.

In table 3.6 is a little cheat sheet of how you can delegate. The one thing I would stress the importance of is that *you still own the outcome*. When you delegate, you're not giving away your responsibility, and therefore you need to stay connected and follow up (trust but verify).

Table 3.6 Delegation cheat sheet

Change your mindset	Establish a routine
As a leader, delegation is one of the most necessary skills. Step one is shifting your mindset to delegate, regardless of how you may feel. It is about empowering and trusting your team. Delegation is not abdication of your responsibility.	Learn how to delegate, being clear on expressing the deliverable/outcome and the purpose/rationale for the task. Accept some trial and error. Spend more time with some people and less with others as you bring them up the learning curve. Utilise other leaders (besides yourself) to support the person doing the task.
Start small	**Trust but verify**
Lower risk delegation first to people you trust. Invite volunteers as they are more likely to be passionate about pleasing you. Gradually expand and take some risks. Allow the team to grow in confidence.	Follow-up is much less work for you than 'doing'. Have a regular but not too frequent approach to follow-up. Coach but don't do or take over. Ask questions to help their learning. Recognise and thank them for their progress.
Accept the result	
Sometimes things will go wrong. Accept it as part of the trade-off that has given you more time. Plus it is a powerful lesson for the team member ... People learn more from failure than success. Don't over-criticise.	

5. There must be consequences

The Accountability Lever 5 is that there must be *consequences*, either positive or negative, for individuals who hit or miss their target.

Why is this important? What you celebrate gets repeated. Those of you who care for children would know that. Praising your child for good behaviour reinforces that behaviour. Not that I'm saying your team are children, but they do like to be recognised for success, particularly by the CEO. Also, what you accept becomes a standard. If you accept people missing their targets, unfortunately that's going to become the norm.

It's also important because failing to deliver against what you promised is a mark of disrespect. This is not the culture you want in a company. A company will never achieve its full potential unless it becomes a high performing, accountable team.

What do I mean by consequences? Think about the sports team leaderboard I mentioned earlier. There are consequences for coming top. A trophy, more TV broadcasts of your games, prize money, a bigger fan base... and as a consequence, more revenue. The consequence of coming last is relegation to a lower-level competition, difficulty attracting high-quality players, smaller crowds, no TV broadcasts, and consequently, less revenue.

In my experience, executing *consequences* is the single most powerful lever of accountability, and often the one where founder CEOs struggle the most. This gap shows up for a few reasons:

- **A blind spot on recognition.** Many leaders are intrinsically motivated and don't care much for recognition themselves. Because of this, they assume it won't matter to others. They overlook how powerful positive consequences, such as recognition, rewards or even simple acknowledgement, can be in reinforcing accountability across a team.

- **Avoidance of conflict.** On the flip side, consequences also mean confronting underperformance. And here's where many leaders, especially inexperienced ones, may suffer. Delivering tough consequences — whether it's a difficult conversation, performance management, or even letting someone go — requires courage to engage. Recall from the trust-building section that handling conflict was one of the critical levers; the same applies here. Many leaders know that it's necessary but delay or avoid it, hoping performance and accountability will improve. But it rarely does if there is no consequence for missing targets.
- **Confusion between fairness and avoidance.** Some founder CEOs hesitate to execute consequences because they don't want to be seen as 'harsh and disrespectful'; not realising that it is possible to have these conversations in a respectful manner.

Accountability doesn't stick unless consequences are consistently applied. Without them, you send a signal that achievement of goals is negotiable and is not a true commitment. When you execute consequences with fairness and respect, you're not only holding individuals accountable, you're role modelling the discipline that is expected across the whole organisation.

In terms of consequences for your teams, there's a full range:

- **Hitting your goals.** The consequences could be a verbal thank you, a WhatsApp or email message, or a small, immaterial gift. Or it could be a high bonus or even a promotion. Any one of these will reinforce the 'consequence of success'.
- **Missing the goal.** This is the other end of the spectrum, and it could be a direct conversation with an individual, such as, 'Hey Janice, you missed delivering that target last week. What happened? I'd really like to know if there is anything I can do to help you'. The next time Janice misses the goal it could be, 'Hey, Janice, this is the second time this has happened. I'm disappointed.

What's going on?' The third or fourth time Janice misses the goal, the consequence could be no bonus for the quarter, or maybe no salary increase at the end of the year. And finally, if Janice misses again, the ultimate consequence could be dismissal.

I will stress again; there must be consequences when people miss the delivery of commitments. Let me share an example from the world of beverage companies, as I once worked for PepsiCo. A Salesperson's goal is higher in summer than it is in winter because people drink more in summer; they are outside more and it is warmer. There is seasonality. However, the proportion of wet weekends versus sunny weekends affects sales, whether it is summer or winter. Despite this, the Salesperson's targets remain the same; they must still achieve them. The leaders of the business cannot accept excuses because, if they do, the company will miss its budget.

Monday reflection

Are you using consequences to embed a culture of accountability? What can you do differently on Monday?

Where leaders struggle with the five levers of accountability

What barriers might stop you from implementing those five levers of accountability? The first, and the most common barrier, is that the leader fails to consistently role-model the right behaviours. I acknowledge this is challenging but it is critical in setting the standard.

The second one could be being too busy to create the targets and the follow-up, and the third might be avoidance of difficult conversations. My answer to these is that there is nothing more important for you than to create a high performing team that delivers against its goals, full stop.

Recall earlier where the first two elements for being a disciplined leader were being *deliberate* in the actions and a *role model* in the behaviours they want their team to copy.

This is another example of discipline beating vision. Without being *deliberate* and a *role model* in your execution of these five levers of accountability, your vision will just remain words on a poster.

Monday ready

In this chapter, you've learned:

- Building trust is the first step towards creating ongoing accountability in your business.
- Trust forms the foundation upon which teams can work together productively and have those tough conversations that move the business towards better decisions and towards its goals. Like Newton's Third Law of Motion, for every action, there is an equal and opposite reaction. If you execute the six levers of trust and the five levers of accountability, you will create a trusting and accountable culture in your business.
- Your results will not change unless you change. You must role-model the right trust and accountability behaviours and be deliberate and disciplined in implementing them.

As mentioned in the previous chapter conclusion, reflect on the list of key takeaways below and focus on two or three changes this Monday. Endeavour to repeat them frequently enough over the next month that they start to become habits. Next month, move on to another two or three changes, and again, endeavour to demonstrate them frequently.

In the next chapter, I'll show you that your company's culture is why people stay and leave the company. If you are not deliberate in creating the culture of your company, it'll be created by others and by default. Its importance demands a deliberate creation.

Key takeaways

Build trust and accountability through disciplined behaviours.
1. Use the trust survey to achieve focus on areas for improvement
2. Six levers to build trust
   - Role-model the right behaviours.
   - Build your emotional intelligence skills.
   - Share information.

- Interact frequently with the leader and the organisation.
- Use trust-building tools.
- Be adept and proactive at handling conflict.

3. Five levers to build accountability
   - Be a role model of accountability.
   - Make clear the deliverables that are expected from your team, and follow up.
   - Ensure visibility of targets and the individual's/team's performance.
   - Delegate with ownership.
   - There must be consequences.

CHAPTER 4

Create a deliberate culture

The company's culture is one of the major reasons people stay or leave your organisation. Even if there are only 20 people in your company, it has an embedded culture and a way of working, whether you were deliberate in its creation or not.

An inspiring *vision* plays a big role in establishing a company's culture but only if it is memorable and is reinforced repeatedly (remember the Taylor Swift analogy from Chapter 2). Similarly, having a set of company *values* can be the foundation for a powerful culture. But again, only if they are remembered and are more than just posters on a wall — they need to be daily filters in your decision making.

This is why discipline beats vision (and values). Having a powerful vision and values is critical to building a great culture but only if you as a disciplined leader are *deliberate* in their communication and use, and you are a constant *role model* of them.

Great culture exists when values lead to the right behaviours, and where those values equal beliefs about what is important and worthwhile in the business. Vision sets direction, but disciplined behaviours embed the values, day after day. Your values must be clear road signs to direct your team, and the filter by which you make decisions. They must be memorable and you must frequently reference them. Ironically, however, most people in companies, even the most senior leaders, can rarely recite all the company's values. Let me illustrate this with a story.

A number of years ago I became CEO of a business in Australia with more than 20 000 employees. On my first day in the role I had a meeting with the 13 members of the leadership team. The first thing we did was introduce ourselves; I gave them all my background and then we went around the table, with each person introducing themselves to me. I then asked, 'Please put your hand up if you know and can recite the four words that are the values of our company. Just be careful if you put your hand up; there's a good chance I'll ask you to tell me those four words'.

Good news: they were all honest. The bad news: only three out of the 13 put their hands up.

All of those people at the table had been with this company for more than five years, and in fact, some for more than 15 years. That boardroom, like many others, had a glass wall so I said to the leadership team, 'Look out the glass window; the values are there on a poster'. They had forgotten they were there, or were just blind to them, as they walk past them every day without seeing them. This situation is not unique. When mentoring CEOs one of the first questions I ask is, 'Can you tell me your company's values?' Sometimes they can, but often, they can't.

The point of this story is, if values are the foundation of the company's culture and if they are the filter by which you make decisions, how on Earth can they have their targeted impact if they're not memorable?

You should care about this because people stay or leave your company because of its culture; they leave when they see leaders who do not operate in line with the company's values or with their own personal values. Staff turnover is costly for many reasons. For example:

1. You lose good people who are productive.
2. You need to recruit new people and those new people are less productive in the first few months.

So turnover is expensive. Therefore, having a poor culture is expensive. The leadership discipline to embed your values every day is what transforms them from a poster on the wall into a sustainable culture. That's why it's discipline, not vision, that determines whether your vision, values and culture become a truly competitive differentiator as you scale.

In this chapter, we will cover the following:

1. Clarify the difference between the company's vision, mission, purpose and values, and understand how they affect your team.
2. Create your company values or, if you already have them, learn how to better embed them into your business.
3. Embed a deliberate culture in your business.
4. Build a culture of recognition, as it is one of your most powerful, and often underutilised, leadership levers.

Purpose, vision, mission and values

Your purpose, vision, mission and values matter — some more than others. They are each different and have varying impacts on the business, as well as varying degrees of longevity. Who you involve in their development also varies; for some, you will want your team heavily involved and they may vote to choose the preferred version. For others, you will want your team involved but it won't be a democracy; you will make the final decision.

Let me clarify each of these by using the hospitality and hotel company, Hyatt, as an example:

- **Purpose statement.** Your purpose statement should reflect why the company exists beyond the product, technology, service or even your financial goals. This statement must pass the test of time and apply to all stakeholders — both internal and external.
  - Hyatt's purpose is 'Caring for the Planet, Caring for People and Caring for Responsible Businesses, every single day'.
  - Analysing this statement, you observe that it is outwardly directed beyond their core business of hotel services provided to their customers, and extends not just to the specific locations of their hotels and customers, but to the world and all people. Their purpose statement is showing their wider all-encompassing care towards the planet we all live on, and all of its inhabitants, which is an ongoing value that will pass the

test of time. This care for the environment and the people of the world, applies to both internal stakeholders of Hyatt, and external customers and corporate clients alike. This can rally the Hyatt team to deliver something impactful to the world and their customers.

- **Vision statement.** The aim of the vision statement is to motivate your team with an aspirational goal on what the company wants to be — its destiny. The vision statement is internally focused and must be memorable. It can change over time as your business and aspiration changes.
  - Hyatt's vision is 'To be the most preferred hospitality company'.
  - This statement is clearly a very aspirational goal as it is targeting global impact. It is also something that all the team can understand and aspire to achieve through their roles. It is similar to the purpose, which creates some alignment between the purpose and vision. It is also short and memorable, so easy for the team to keep it top of mind.

- **Mission statement.** This is the who, what, how and why of the business. It is an action-oriented statement.
  - Hyatt's mission is 'To care for people so they can be their best'.
  - This statement has similarities to the purpose and vision but is a statement that is more about the 'how' than the vision and purpose statements and is clearly an action statement. The action here is to 'care', and it is now a specific kind of internally-focused action on a more specific target, rather than something very broad and visionary — in Hyatt's case, I would imagine they mean to care for their customers, so they can be their best during their stay with Hyatt Hotels.

- **Values.** Values underwrite the purpose. The entire company must sign up for these values. They're necessary to attract and retain your team. You see them all over the company: on walls, on boards, in your annual report and in your presentations to investors. They are the umbrella over how the company operates.

They rarely change. Examples of values are honesty, integrity, innovation, accountability, teamwork, safety first, transparency and customer focus.

Purpose, vision and values are the most critical and matter the most to the company, while mission, arguably, matters the least. Why? Well, purpose is critical as it's often why people joined the company, and why they stay. They align with whatever the company is trying to achieve, a goal beyond financial targets. Purpose doesn't change unless the company's product or service changes. Vision is an aspirational and motivational goal that the team want to achieve. It inspires them to crash through walls to achieve it. This can change over time as aspirations expand or your business varies its direction. Values are the road signs that direct people towards what is most important in how the company operates. Values guide the team on behaviour and decision making, and these should rarely change.

Statements of a company's mission describe what it does, and seldom have the motivational power of the company's vision, values and purpose. The mission often focuses on *what* and *how*, which evolve as the company grows. In many cases, the company's mission and purpose are most similar. The mission is probably the one that will change the most as your company develops. Therefore, it's likely to be the least needed in the early stages of your company's evolution.

Why should you care about purpose, vision and values, and why bother to create them?

1. **Organisational alignment.** A clear vision provides a long-term direction for the company, ensuring all team members are working towards common goals to achieve this aspirational target. The values guide decision making and behaviour across the organisation, reducing misalignment, and ensuring the company does things the right way.

2. **Employee engagement.** A meaningful purpose motivates and commits employees because they understand their work's

contribution. Millennials and Gen Z often prioritise purpose and values over financial incentives. They want to work for a company whose purposes align with their own personal agendas.

3. **Customer loyalty.** A well-articulated purpose resonates with customers, building trust and connections. Companies with strong values and purpose often attract loyal customers who align with their vision.

Some of you reading this might be thinking, 'I'm not sure I agree. We have a results-oriented culture. Some of these things, like vision, purpose and values, are more intangible, softer and more difficult to measure. I want my company to be results-oriented and focused on actual outcomes that we can measure'. You might also think that you've seen many companies that talk about purpose and values, which seems inauthentic because the leaders don't operate in line with those values, and the company doesn't deliver aligned with its purpose.

Although I can accept those as reasonable arguments, there is a wealth of research — which I will share with you as this chapter progresses — that shows the significant return on investment (ROI) for any company of having and focusing on a strong purpose, a clear vision and powerful values.

Values as the foundation for your culture

Your values are the core of your culture, shaping the decisions, behaviours and priorities that define how your company operates. However, your values are ineffective as guides for decision making if people do not remember them.

Let me tell you another story about the same group that I mentioned earlier. Our values were entrepreneurship, quality, responsibility and honesty. Fortunately, I had a talented HR leader, and he and his team experimented with those words and changed the order to honesty, entrepreneurship and responsibility, and renamed the fourth value to *our* quality — creating the acronym HERO. We then used that as a term for our employees: our HEROs. We used the term 'HERO' many, many times a day in the full range of communication from leadership team meetings to all-hands meetings, to my weekly CEO messages.

When I joined the company, only three out of the 13 leadership team members knew the four values. By the time I left five years later — because of the HERO acronym and many initiatives — 95 per cent of our 800 white-collar workers and more than 60 per cent of our 20 000 front-line workers knew our four values of honesty, entrepreneurship and responsibility, as well as our quality. Your values must be memorable for them to play a critical part in the culture of your company.

Does that mean everyone who remembered those four words operated and lead with them in mind? Not necessarily. However, step one in embedding your values is the team knowing what they are.

Monday reflection

How many members of your team can remember and recite your values? How can you make your values memorable? Is it possible to re-order them and create an acronym?

Now, some of you might dispute this idea that values are too abstract and too soft. My response is that there are many studies that confirm the positive impact of these concepts. One was an extensive study by consultants McKinsey in 2024, in which their research across 1000+ organisations around the world confirmed that those with values-based cultures produced 60 per cent higher total shareholder returns and significantly outpaced their peers in revenue growth.

Another pushback sometimes raised by founder CEOs is to question whether these values truly change behaviour, as they are only words. I can accept that argument, if that is the case. However, as a disciplined leader, your role is to be *deliberate* in translating these words into actions, and to *role-model* the values with your behaviours and the decisions that you and your team make.

The following suggestions are intended to help you, as leaders, to create your company's purpose, vision and values.

1. Purpose

Hold an offsite with your leadership team. The CEO should begin by sharing the story behind the company's origination and talk about the products and services you offer. Following your introduction, ask each team member to answer these questions:

- Why does our business exist beyond making money?
- Who are our customers?
- What problem are we solving, or what value are we creating for our customers?
- How does our business impact the community, industry or world at large?
- What significant change or benefit is our company bringing to the world?

Collect input from the leadership group and place it on a whiteboard. Invest time as a team in evaluating these answers and endeavour to choose the most powerful and accurate answer to *each* of the questions. Now the difficult part: choose a purpose statement that reflects these answers. There may be someone in the group who sees a purpose statement quickly, or you could use AI to assist with options. Once you have one or a few statements, reflect on them over a month or two. Survey other stakeholders for their input.

It's important to get this right. It must resonate with internal and external stakeholders, so must be simple, inspiring and memorable for the team and customers alike.

2. Vision

Identify the company's long-term destination. The vision should stretch your team's ambition while being achievable. While it's broad and aspirational, it's also important that you can identify some tangible milestones over time that assist you in measuring progress towards that goal. The vision might be a narrow statement that focuses on your customers or your industry, or it could be far broader, expanding the comparison to beyond your industry. For example, do you aspire to be 'the most popular and profitable movie company in Australia', or, 'the most popular and profitable company in the entertainment industry in the southern hemisphere', or even, 'the most popular and profitable digital content company in the world'?

Ask questions like:

- What would success look like for your business in the future and how is it measured? Is it customer reputation, impact on society or market share? Is it revenue and profitability, or employee engagement, or disruption and re-creation of an industry?
- Where do you want your business to be in five, ten or 20 years? Can you articulate the key measures or milestones you could target at a point in time in the future? These targets might be market share, revenue, brand regard, employee engagement and retention.
- How do you see the impact of your business evolving over time? Do you want a three-year vision, knowing you will need to create another vision at that point? Or do you want a goal that is ten years away?

There is no right answer to the above questions, only what you think will be an aspirational and tangible goal that will motivate the team.

Similarly to the development of your purpose, once you have chosen a vision statement, you can collect input from the leadership group and stakeholders to ensure it resonates with everyone. Circulate and obtain feedback. Do not make a hasty decision. Sit with it and reflect for a few months before locking it in. In my experience, this is not a democracy. You, as the founder CEO, will have the final say.

3. Values

Start by having each person communicate their own two personal values (no more) and what experiences in their lives shaped those values. It can help to ask them what leader or company they admire and why. This

Table 4.1 Most used company values

Accountability	Creativity	Facilitation	Involvement	Recognition
Adventure	Curiosity	Faith	Justice	Renewal
Agility	Customer-Centric	Family	Knowledge	Respect
Appreciation	Courage	Forgiveness	Leadership	Responsibility
Authenticity	Determination	Freedom	Learning	Security
Balance	Development	Friendship	Love	Self-respect
Boldness	Diversity	Fun	Loyalty	Speed
Caring	Effectiveness	Generosity	Openness	Strength
Challenge	Empathy	Gratitude	Order	Success
Change	Encouragement	Growth	Ownership	Sustainability
Collaboration	Endurance	Harmony	Passion	Teamwork
Cooperation	Entrepreneurial	Honesty	Peace	Transparency
Compassion	Excellence	Humour	Pride	Trust
Connection	Excitement	Innovation	Professionalism	Truth
Contentment		Instinct	Quality	Wellness
		Integrity	Reciprocity	Wisdom

sets the foundation to create values that resonate with the entire team. Refer to the list of potential values in table 4.1. These are 80 of the most popular values elected by corporations. Have each person in your team look at the list and choose three or four that resonate most with them in the context of your business.

Put them all on a whiteboard or on the wall with Post-it notes and let the team debate and agree on the six values that best align with the organisation and its goals. However, this is not a democracy; you as the leader should have the final say.

Ideally, you should have only three, or maybe four, values. Let those values sit with the team for three months, with regular reflection in the leadership team meetings on how these values are guiding decisions. Socialise the values with the broader team. After about three months, lock them in with broad organisational communication. Again, your values must be memorable. Avoid using long sentences or descriptors, as people won't remember them. It's most powerful to create an acronym, like we did with HERO.

After finalising your values and the acronym, hold a leadership team meeting to determine the initiatives required to embed those values.

Founder story

Sam was in the education space, and was proud that he and his team had created a set of values along with a vision and purpose statement around five years ago.

Following a conversation I had with him on the impact his values were having on the business, he asked his leadership team to articulate the company's values and how they use them in what they do. Unfortunately, no member of his team could recall more than two of the four values, and half of them could not remember the purpose statement.

At his next retreat we worked on initiatives to more deeply embed his values in the business (see template below).

Monday reflection

What are the actions and behaviours your team can frequently and consistently execute to better embed your company values? Use the template in table 4.2.

Table 4.2 Values and initiatives to embed (example template)

Value	Initiatives to embed
Students first: We are here to serve our students.	• Use this as a question to filter our decisions at our leadership meetings. • Embed the message by continually using this phrase in all-hands meetings and tell stories where we have done this.

(continued)

Table 4.2 (continued)

Value	Initiatives to embed
We are students: We focus on our development.	• Talk about continuous learning frequently in the organisation. • Send 'teaching' messages each week to the organisation by rolling LT responsibility, quotes, interesting articles, etc. • We each own our development.
Honesty and respect: Be honest and respectful in all communications.	• Ask this question at the end of each meeting: Were we honest and respectful in this meeting?
Do what we say: We walk the talk.	• Ask this question at the end of each week: Did I do what I said I would do this week?

I would suggest that you re-do the template each year at your strategy retreat to ensure that you continue to embed your values with fresh ideas and initiatives.

Discipline does beat vision. However, an inspiring vision, a powerful purpose, and clear values to which the team are committed, are critical components of your business's success. Don't underestimate the need for them.

Creating a deliberate culture

The third topic in this chapter is creating a deliberate culture. This is a critical responsibility for you as the leader and is too important to leave to chance.

So, what is culture? One useful way to describe it is, 'Culture is what people do when you are not looking'. Another is, 'Culture is how things are done around here'. Either way, your culture is the reason people stay — or leave — your company. It is the sum of values, norms, beliefs and behaviours demonstrated by you and your team. And as leader, you set the tone, constantly sending signals about which behaviours are acceptable, and therefore, about the culture itself.

Every choice you make reinforces this; the people you recruit, how you onboard them, the training you provide, who you spend time with, how you recognise and reward contributions, who you promote or dismiss, and even how you allocate time in your calendar. Each of these decisions sends a signal about your company's culture. Senior leadership must be *deliberate* and ensure that words, symbols and actions align consistently with the culture you are trying to create.

You might think culture is difficult to measure, but one of the clearest indicators is staff turnover. Companies with strong, healthy cultures retain people longer and attract top talent simply because they are places where people want to work.

You can also measure culture through tools like employee surveys — especially the Employee Net Promoter Score (eNPS), which shows the percentage of people who would recommend your company as a great place to work. Think about today's most admired companies; their reputations extend beyond products or profits. What people most often say is that they are great places to work. When you build such a culture, attracting and retaining talent becomes easier, your customers want to engage with you, and your returns will follow.

How can you create a *deliberate* culture? As I mentioned previously, everything you do as the CEO impacts culture. However, below is a more focused list of suggestions, grouped by category, of how you and your team can be disciplined in the creation and articulation of a deliberate culture for your business.

1. Define your culture

Step one to creating a deliberate culture is being able to describe what you want it to look like in five or six sentences. To start, write answers to the below questions:

1. What are your purpose and vision?
2. What are your values? Articulate each of these in a sentence that provides context to the value. For example, instead of 'Innovation', say: 'We experiment and fail fast. We want a new product idea each week, knowing only 5 per cent will get to market'.
3. What style of leadership do you need in the business to achieve these goals? For example, 'We expect leaders to be direct but respectful. The leaders and their team must honestly communicate their opinions'. Or, 'Our leaders set the example in terms of customer mania. They are in the field with customers over 50 per cent of each week'.
4. What types of people do we need in the business for us to be successful? For example, 'We want maximum demographic diversity to understand all points of view'. 'We need people who speak up honestly and who listen respectfully'. 'We need people who are 100 per cent behind our vision and our purpose, and whose values align with those of the company'.
5. What trade-offs are we prepared to make? For example, you may need the business to move extremely quickly, so a trade-off may be that you will make decisions with over 70 per cent of the information as accumulating 90 per cent will take too long.
6. Identify specific actions or rituals that are done to send powerful messages about the company. For example, I read that in the early days of Amazon, Jeff Bezos used doors on boxes as desks to illustrate the frugality of the business. Think about other norms in your company that send a signal about how you and your team operate.

The above is a baseload of questions for you to reflect on to be able to articulate the key elements you are targeting with the company's culture. (Remember, the earlier insight into that culture is 'How we do things around here'.) Over time this will coalesce into a five-to-seven sentence description of your company's culture.

Now that you can describe what type of culture you want and need, how do you ensure that your actions deliberately build it and reinforce it?

2. Consider your people and processes

Hiring: The people joining the company must fit your culture. Go deep into interviews, understand the candidate, understand what their values are and ask multiple people to interview candidates and allow veto votes if someone feels the candidate is not right. Have fixed probation periods and dismiss if they are the wrong fit, regardless of performance.

Onboarding, and training and development: Orientation that educates on the company's values and the culture that exists. Involve key leaders with standard presentations to ensure consistency and alignment with your purpose, vision and values. Ongoing training and development also must be aligned with your desired culture. For example, if one of your values is personal growth, then consider how much the company is investing in supporting the team in their growth. Do you provide in-house training or fund external training?

Resources and investments: Are you investing people and cash in areas that align with your culture? This is very visible to the team and will be noticed if that is not the case.

3. Look at your structure, pay and performance incentives

Organisation structure: The way you organise your company must re-enforce your targeted culture. If your passion is supporting the customer, does the organisation reflect this? For example, how far away are you from the customer? Early in your company journey, it will be one level. However, as your company scales, how many layers of people are between you and the customer?

Rewards: Pay for performance but balance with base salary, short-term incentive, long-term incentive and profit sharing, and also evaluate people based on their alignment with the company's values. Performance metrics that are put up and shared also reinforce — or undermine — the company's culture. Make bonus and pay calculations transparent.

Promotions: Are the people you are promoting great examples of your company's desired culture? If not, then the organisation will notice and judge you on your commitment to the company's culture.

4. Share information

Information sharing affects the culture. Your own stories as the founder CEO embed the culture. What information you share also strengthens or weakens your culture. For example, recall that in Chapter 2 we looked at how sharing information builds trust. If your desired culture is to have an empowered team, then they need the information to do their jobs. Withholding information therefore undermines your culture.

5. Consider job design

Your workplace has a significant impact on the company's culture. Do you want a flexible culture? Do you want a more rigid culture? Is it office versus home? How much are you leveraging technology? The workplace that is aligned with a desired culture inspires or encourages interactions.

6. Assess your leadership

Your leadership and that of your team: Is it visible? Are you accessible? Are you consistent? Do you emphasise the values? Consider the culture that you desire for the company and reflect on whether you and your leadership team are reinforcing it or diminishing it.

Your calendar: If someone analysed your calendar, would they agree it aligned with your company's targeted culture? If you say your company puts customers first, how much time do you actually spend with them?

There are at least another 20 areas that I could mention. However, hopefully the above suggestions are sufficient as a template to show you how thoughtful you must be in creating a powerful and deliberate culture.

The template in table 4.3 is also useful as a reminder on how to impact culture.

Table 4.3 Levers to impact culture

Culture	You	Your team
Must be able to articulate what it is and why it is a strength for the business.	Your authentic leadership shadow is one of the major drivers of company culture.	The whole team must reflect the company values, every day.
Communication	**Values**	**Recruitment**
Everyone must know and understand the values and your company culture. Use stories to embed.	Have a concise list of the values that provide the roadmap or filter by which the company operates. Have an acronym to help memorability.	Have a clear process with standards/templates for recruitment.
Orientation	**Recognition**	**Crises**
After the first day they must go home and say 'I made a great decision joining this company!'	Should be formal and informal. The people you recognise must also be role models for your values.	This is when people will watch you most intently to see your consistency with values and culture.

Why might you struggle to do the above? If you haven't established purpose, vision and values yet in your business, then you do have a lot to do. However, it is worth the journey and it is essential to create a deliberate culture.

The power of recognition

The fourth topic of this chapter is recognition. Recognition is your most powerful and most accurate, but often the most underutilised, leadership lever.

Let me tell you a story. If you recall early in the chapter, I mentioned the HERO acronym for the company's values. To help embed these values, we created a CEO HERO award. The trophies were indeed HERO awards, featuring miniature figurines of Superman and Wonder Woman.

Over a five-year period I gave out over 200 of these CEO HERO awards to people who reflected the company's values. Most of the time I would provide them to our front-line team members, but I also gave them to our office staff. I thoroughly enjoyed giving them out and always received a positive response from the recipient as they appreciated being recognised and 'being seen' by the company CEO.

Such recognition is powerful. I remember one day I was in my office when a divisional president came in and told me that, unfortunately, one of his team members — let's call him Josh — had passed away tragically from a brain aneurysm. This was very sad news as Josh was a valued and well-respected team member, and had been with the company for 23 years. At the funeral I walked down the middle aisle, stepped into a pew and then looked up at the coffin. I saw something on the coffin and my heart missed a beat. The service started and Josh's brother stood up to do the eulogy. He explained that Josh loved his time with our company, then took a few steps forward, reached over and picked up the HERO award that was on top of the coffin. He held it up and said, 'Josh's proudest day was when the CEO gave him this award'. Now, it doesn't happen often that you give out an award and it is identified at someone's funeral, but it does validate the massive power of recognition.

Founder story

Alice was a very intelligent, strategic and hard-driving founder. Her team respected her immensely for her intellect, passion and ability to chart the best way forward for the company. A gap in her leadership, however, was that she rarely thanked or complimented her team. This was mainly because she didn't need compliments herself.

After performing a 360-degree feedback survey on her, the team gave clear feedback. They indicated that they loved working with her but were frustrated and a little demotivated as they were never acknowledged or thanked, no matter how hard they worked or what they achieved.

On receiving this feedback, Alice made a number of immediate changes, including:

- putting a simple prompt in her calendar to remind her to recognise someone each Tuesday and Friday. After a month she removed these reminders.
- adding into her weekly team meetings agenda a 'call out' so that she and other members of the team had the opportunity to specifically thank and recognise other team members.

The impact was almost immediate. Although the team knew this was not natural for Alice, it did become authentic, and the team greatly appreciated this change.

Monday reflection

What recognition and appreciation can you implement, starting Monday?

The research behind recognition

I have been to hundreds of recognition events and have found that almost every single time, I saw more emotion than you can imagine. Recognition works. Independent of my experience, there is a huge amount of research.

- In a 2023 Gallup–Workhuman study titled 'From Praise to Profits', organisations that doubled the number of employees receiving weekly recognition saw a 9 per cent boost in productivity, 22 per cent fewer safety incidents, and 22 per cent less absenteeism.
- A May 2024 Gallup study found employees who receive high-quality recognition are 45 per cent less likely to leave within two years.

Recognition is not soft and fluffy. Recognition has tangible returns to keep people appreciated and engaged, and as a result they stay longer.

How to recognise people

There are a few principles that I'd start with. Number one is to recognise great work and ideas. It might be a simple call out in a team meeting, 'Hey, I'd like to thank person X for that great idea'. It might be sending someone an email or a WhatsApp. Maybe you copy people in, maybe you don't.

Second, make it fun. David Novak, the founding CEO of Yum! Brands, which is the global owner of KFC, Pizza Hut and Taco Bell, was an amazing inspirational leader. One of his key planks for driving team engagement and company profitability was recognition. I learned most of my recognition skills from David, and they served me well in my life and career. One thing he would say was 'Make recognition fun and make it personal'. I encourage you to read his book, *Taking People with You*.

Below are a few suggestions on what you can do to embed a recognition culture.

1. Informal actions
    - Respond to every email. If you are the CEO, when someone emails you, they're waiting for a response. A simple, 'Thank you, I've got it' or 'Thank you, appreciated'. This is small, but just responding to people makes a difference. Think about when you were younger and you emailed your boss. You were always waiting for a response.
    - Give a 'Well done and thank you' when someone has achieved something significant or they've achieved a goal you had set them. Maybe it's a handwritten card, maybe it's an email. What I would suggest you do is put a little Post-it note above your monitor and target to recognise someone on a Tuesday and Friday each week. It's easy to do.
    - During weekly all-hands meetings or team calls, always find a reason to recognise someone. Now, it can't be fake and inauthentic. There has to be a solid reason for the recognition, and it needs to be for something specific. Know the person's name and be specific for the reason.
    - If your organisation has a lot of operations, when you visit a site, make sure you recognise someone on site. Ask the site manager who you should recognise.
2. Formal actions
    - In your CEO newsletter always include some recognition. Acknowledge one of the team members.
    - Set up a formal program, such as a team member of the month award.
    - There could be awards for top Salesperson of the week or the month.
    - Annual awards at your annual dinner are also extremely powerful in motivating people. Make them fun and entertaining.

Why might you find this difficult to do? It can be awkward and unnatural for you, which I can understand. What I can say, however, is that it changes over time. Start small, make this a habit. There are so many studies that confirm recognition has a huge payback; and I am sure you will enjoy it!

Monday ready

In conclusion, your team are inspired by the company's vision, purpose and values, however the company's culture is the reason people stay, and often why they leave.

If you are not *deliberate* and disciplined in creating the culture of your company, others will create it. It's too important to be randomly created. Your company's values are the foundation, so be structured in how you create them, as well as the vision and the purpose. Finally, create a recognition culture. It'll give you higher employee engagement and retention, and overall better business performance. Your ROI from recognition will be significant, I can assure you of that.

The thing you need to do first is to identify the purpose, vision and values for the company. Use the matrix provided to identify initiatives that can embed your values.

Remember my suggestion in Chapter 3. Focus on only two or three changes this Monday and endeavour to repeat them frequently enough over the next month that they start to become habits. Then next month, move onto another two or three changes, and again endeavour to demonstrate them frequently. Use the list below as a template to map your targeted changes over the first two months.

In the next chapter, I will show you approaches you can use to mentor and develop your team because, as leader, the team looks to you to develop and support them. They expect you to invest time with them. Over time, this will likely become one of your proudest achievements.

Key takeaways

Create a deliberate culture.
1. Disciplined and impactful behaviours.
   - What will you start doing (or do more of)?
   - What will you stop doing (or do less of)?
2. Identify your company's purpose, vision and values.

3. Determine initiatives to embed your values using the template in table 4.2.
4. Build a deliberate culture and be disciplined in your actions to reinforce, not undermine, your culture.
5. Embed a recognition culture with informal and formal initiatives.

CHAPTER 5

Develop your team's discipline

Whether or not you want the responsibility, your team looks to you to develop them. The team members respect you and want to learn from you as their leader. They expect you to invest time with them on a regular basis. You may devote this time to problem solving technical issues, teaching impactful leadership behaviours, or addressing personal issues such as handling the stress of balancing a demanding job and a young family. Choosing to approach this responsibility with discipline and structure is what ensures your team grows alongside you as the business scales up.

Over time, one of your proudest achievements will be seeing your team develop, and even leave to become founders of their own companies. I loved this opportunity to mentor my team and am proud of the leaders I've influenced in their careers. This reinforces the core message of this book: vision inspires people to join, but discipline in developing them keeps them engaged, learning and staying with the company.

Recall that: *A disciplined leader is deliberate, self-aware, and consistently role-models the behaviours they expect from others. They are a relentless student, constantly evolving their leadership approaches and reinventing themselves as new challenges arise or as the business requires.*

Each of these elements is relevant to how you grow your team. Specifically:

1. You need to be *deliberate* in your approach to developing your team.
2. Your *self-awareness and role modelling* are multiplicative behaviours and will be copied by your team. Remember the concept of the leadership shadow in Chapter 2.
3. Being a *relentless student* will be copied by your team. You will need to continuously learn new ways to support and grow your team as the business increases its complexity.

This chapter is about the approaches you can implement, starting Monday, to develop your team. Then, in Chapter 6 I'll share with you how to maximise impact through powerful communication techniques, because your impact is more than just the words you use — more on that later.

Many leaders get confused about the difference between these three leadership duties: providing feedback to the team on KPIs, performing appraisals and mentoring leaders.

- A **KPI discussion** centres on the review of an individual's or team's performance against their targets, determining the necessary adjustments to overcome any shortfall and ensure that the individual, function or division contributes to the company achieving its goal. This discussion could be progress on a specific initiative, or some other targeted outcome, such as a particular customer account or a financial metric.
- A **performance appraisal** is best held twice a year, focusing on critical leadership behaviours, potentially identified through a 360 review or from your observations as the boss. You might use a performance development plan (PDP) as a tool to document the gaps and opportunities — or the appraisal may be unstructured, although this is not ideal.

- A **mentoring program** is a longer investment with regular sessions to support the personal growth of an individual you select because of their potential within your company. This individual may be one of your direct reports, or a high-potential leader who is currently lower in the organisation.

Without commitment and structure these conversations happen too sporadically or with limited direction. Your discipline is what transforms feedback, appraisals and mentoring from tick-box exercises into engines of growth for your team and, consequently, for the business.

You may feel that you are too busy and can delegate or outsource this responsibility because you feel your other priorities are more important. However, as the business grows and the challenges of scaling become more complex, developing your team is a critical lever for the business's success. Also, through mentoring your team and the people in the levels below them, you gain greater insight into their competency, helping you to understand whether they can grow their skills at the same pace as your scaling business. Better to find this out sooner rather than later.

You don't need to rely on my perspective here, as there is substantial research showing this is a critical part of your role and adds tremendous value to the performance of the company. A 2023 *Forbes* article citing research by MetrixGlobal found that executive coaching delivers a 788 per cent ROI, mainly through increased productivity and improved retention. Similarly, PwC's 2025 Global Coaching Survey found organisations reported an average 7 times return on their coaching investment, with some reporting as high as 10 to 49 times their investment.

In this chapter, we'll cover how to hold the three critical performance and development conversations:

- KPI tracking meetings
- structured performance appraisals
- intentional mentoring of young leaders.

I will also provide you with an approach to obtain feedback from your team because, as the founder CEO, it's challenging to get feedback on where you can improve. Your team will be cautious in giving you honest performance feedback.

KPI tracking meetings

You *must* hold regular meetings with your key staff about how they are tracking against their KPIs. This section could have been included in Chapter 3 where I shared Accountability Lever 2 (*Make clear the deliverables expected from your team and follow up relentlessly*). However, it belongs in this chapter because I see KPI meetings as an extremely powerful approach to develop your team.

Being disciplined in guiding your team to hit these weekly, monthly or quarterly targets provides learning moments for them. In addition, these are the essential micro-steps to follow to build to your vision. Here again we see that discipline beats vision.

As the renowned management consultant and author Peter Drucker said, 'What gets measured gets done'. I would extend this sentence, with some creative grammar, to, 'What gets measured, *and bonused*, gets done'.

Tracking and measuring objectives, with regular follow-up, focuses attention and effort on what is most important, and therefore leads to outcomes that are aligned with the company's goal. Remember the quote I shared in Chapter 3, 'Trust but verify'; these KPI meetings verify progress and allow you the opportunity to support and coach your team on how they can hit their targets.

These sessions could be quick check-ins of less than 15 minutes or they can be longer meetings. Either way, the session must cover performance against the KPIs, and include what may need to change to close a gap.

Performance against KPIs is the most accurate and real-time evaluation of a product, division or function's performance. As we covered in Chapter 3, there must be consequences for that performance; both positive and negative.

The optimum approach to talk about performance against KPIs is to first invest the time to create crystal clear targets — ideally inputs and outcomes. The KPI discussions should be regular and scheduled — every two weeks at a minimum — with a focus on the individual's or team's performance against the targets, and including the documenting of actions completed and, more importantly, of future plans to close any gaps to increase the certainty of hitting the targets.

To complement the catch-ups, include deeper dive reviews each quarter. In these sessions, it would be appropriate for the division or function to bring their key leaders to present to you and the leadership team. Like the catch-ups, be sure to document the outcomes of these quarterly KPI meetings, focusing on actions to maintain momentum and close any gaps versus their commitments.

At the end of the year, the individual and team KPI performances must feed into bonus payouts and salary increases. Recall that 'What gets measured, *and bonused*, gets done'. There is no doubt that a monetary implication for hitting or missing targets amplifies individuals' focus on hitting their targets. But you don't need to believe just me — the co-founder of Berkshire Hathaway, Charlie Munger, once said, 'I think I've been in the top five per cent of my age cohort all my life in understanding the power of incentives, and all my life I've underestimated that power'.

It takes time to develop the KPIs and then hold these regular meetings, but you will see dramatic results, in real-time focus on critical targets, in higher employee engagement, and ultimately in better business outcomes. In addition, by *role modelling* this approach to the team you will almost certainly lead them to copy you and do the same with their own teams, helping to creating a culture of accountability.

Founder story

Ranjiv was immensely frustrated with the performance of his sales leader and the sales team, as each month the business missed the revenue budget.

His approach had been to sit with the sales leader in December each year to agree the monthly targets that built to the annual target. He would then review the disappointing shortfall with the sales manager at the end of each month.

He had limited time to focus on sales because the majority of his time was taken up by:

- working with the CTO and engineers. Because he was an engineer himself, he felt he could add the most value here in taking the product to the next level.
- account managing the three largest accounts. He had a strong relationship with these customers who provided 60 per cent of his company's revenue, and they only wanted to deal with Ranjiv.
- responding to the board, who were extremely demanding of his time.

After discussion, Ranjiv realised there were a number of reasons for the sales shortfall but the biggest was that, although the sales manager knew the product and had great relationship skills, he had no structure or process for managing the sales team.

Over a four-month period Ranjiv did three things that had a positive impact:

1. He worked with the sales manager to cascade the annual and monthly company targets into monthly sales targets by product for each sales rep. He also initiated fortnightly

> KPI meetings with the sales team, diving deep into progress against each sales opportunity.
> 2. He increased the commission percentage to the sales reps, including individual and team payouts if targets were hit each month.
> 3. He increased his time out in the field, visiting and selling to potential customers. His presence was a powerful sales tool, and he was also able to better evaluate and train the sales team.
>
> Six months after starting the above, the company started to hit its targets, and then continued to achieve them.

Monday reflection

Does your sales team have detailed monthly sales targets broken down by product and geography, and customer segment? Is their progress reviewed at least every two weeks by the sales leader and, potentially, by you? Is your commission structure driving individual and team collaboration to hit targets?

A final thought on why these KPI meetings are so important: some ineffective leaders simply tell their team to 'Just do it', providing limited or no assistance in how to achieve the target. Being a disciplined leader requires you to guide and advise your team. This means they are more likely to hit their target and grow as leaders with your guidance.

Structured performance appraisals

Excuse my language, but the 's...t sandwich' works in a performance appraisal and development discussion if you follow my approach.

The so-called 's…t sandwich' is used to describe a feedback approach where the leader first gives the individual positive feedback, then gives the negative (the 's…t') in the middle, and finishes with more positive feedback. The secret ingredient to make this feedback successful is making it a two-way conversation focused on the exact behaviours that are, and are not, working.

I remember bumping into someone I hadn't seen in about 15 years at an event recently. We had a conversation about where she is today and what she's doing. Out of the blue, she said, 'Hey, Dane, I still have all those appraisals you went through with me. I've kept them in a folder'. I laughed and said, 'Why did you keep them?' She replied, 'They were a great guide for me in the right behaviours as a leader, and even the bad stuff was good for me to remember. I keep them and refer to them occasionally'.

This was not a unique conversation. Many people I've worked with tell me they still have their performance appraisals and the feedback I'd given them.

Recall Chapter 2 and the concept of the *leadership shadow*; you have immense positional power. People remember the time you invested in them to grow them as leaders. As the founder CEO of the business, this is something you must be good at. The team expects it, and deserves the feedback. If you don't develop them within the company, they will leave to find an organisation that will grow them.

You might think, 'No-one ever coached me, and I did okay'. Well first, you don't know what opportunities you missed from not getting feedback. You may have developed even faster as a leader if you had received feedback. Second, just because it wasn't important for you, doesn't mean your team doesn't want or need it.

How to deliver a performance appraisal

Use the approach described below to deliver a performance appraisal. Invest the time to write your planned discussion, and break it into two sections:

1. **What I appreciate about you.** In this first section, write the four or five positive leadership behaviours you observe the individual performing, including examples of these behaviours. Some examples of 'appreciates' could be:
   - Your inclusive approach to problem solving with your team has led to increased collaboration within your team, and better decisions, versus a year ago. Several people have made this comment to me.
   - Your presentation skills have improved over the last six months since I raised this in your last appraisal. You appear less nervous, engaging more with the audience, and the presentations are clearer in their messaging.
   - You have shown great accountability in delivering Project X on time, as I know there were many significant challenges to overcome.
   - I appreciate your customer focus and that you have increased the time you are spending in the field meeting with our customers. It is making a difference, as shown by the higher customer retention rates that your division is achieving.
2. **How you can be more effective.** In this second section document the ineffective or missing behaviours that the leader should use. Some examples of how they could be more effective might be:
   - You can become defensive in our leadership team meetings when one of your peers, or me, challenges what you are saying. The discussion then becomes aggressive and, sometimes, personal. Be open to others' views.
   - You have two very talented team members who need more of your time to mentor and develop them. They have potential but need your guidance.

Ensure you identify at least two more points of appreciation than effective behaviours. People count and remember the number of each. If you have more 'effectives' than 'appreciates', the individual will recognise that and possibly feel disheartened. I understand that as you read this, it feels rigged and disingenuous. However, I know this approach works.

Table 5.1 is an example document that I created for one of my leaders.

Table 5.1 Feedback template

What I appreciate	How you can be more effective
• Seeing you at all-hands meetings, you have noticeably improved your presence up front and the clarity of what you say. • You have handled the pressure of the role very well over the last 6 months. Your calmness and control are powerful role modelling for your team to see. • You are proactive in getting ahead of the curve on profit improvement plans. • You are building a strong team with some excellent new additions.	• Be more open to feedback. At times you can become defensive or explain it away. This behaviour is also happening in our leadership team meetings when someone challenges you. • I understand that you are busy; however, you need to spend more time in the field visiting customers and our front-line team.

Another story for you — when I was working with Yum! Brands I spent three months working in a KFC restaurant prior to being sent to South Africa to run the KFC business there. I trained as a store manager and learned that, when working with teenage staff members and training them, you need to be specific about what you want them to do. For example, if you tell a 15-year-old to clean the dining area, you must be specific. For example, tell them to 'Clear the table, wipe any excess scraps from the table, spray disinfectant on the table and wipe it clean with one of the blue rags. Do the same with the chairs. Then sweep the floor and mop it with the black mop and use the green disinfectant in the bucket'. You must be specific about what you want them to do and the order in which to do it.

Now, I am not suggesting that your team are like 15-year-olds, however in your appraisals you must be specific about the behaviours you want the leader to replicate in terms of the elements within 'What I appreciate', and what you need them to change as articulated in the 'How to be more effective' section.

In the conversation, don't let them read ahead. If having the discussion in person, I would have a piece of paper and slide it down line by line to keep them focused on the point we're discussing. At the end of the journey, give them the piece of paper to take away. If it's a Zoom call, use a box that hides what you are not discussing and drag the box down to share each new point. After the conversation, email them the full document. It's important that they take this away, and you should offer them the opportunity to come back for another discussion if there are things they want reinforced or clarified.

In the conversation, use the word 'and' not 'but' when transitioning from what you appreciate to areas in which they can improve. Say, 'You are showing a lot of really positive behaviours, *and* there are areas where you can be more effective in your leadership'.

This is *not* a KPI discussion. This focuses on the leadership behaviours you want to see more of, and those areas that need improvement. To complement this approach, the individual may have a PDP. A PDP talks about competencies they need to improve and what their job aspirations are. It is a useful part of the performance appraisal process. For startup businesses with fewer than 50 people, I wouldn't go down the PDP route. Talking about what you appreciate and how they can be more effective is a better investment of your time, early on.

A performance appraisal does not always need to be as structured as above. If the individual is performing poorly, then don't fake it with the 'What I appreciates'. Be honest and direct with the team member and go straight to what needs to be improved. If you have given this critical feedback before, and no change has been made, you will need to decide whether this is a final warning for improvement prior to dismissal. Recall the Chapter 3 discussion on the need for 'consequences' to create a culture of accountability.

Some leaders struggle with the above early on due to a lack of confidence, especially if they don't have experience in communicating this sort of appraisal. If you follow the above scripts and the process, your confidence will build. There will be times when individuals you are appraising focus heavily on the negative aspects, but as you repeatedly do this each quarter or half-year, you will find that rapport builds and you have more and more effective discussions with them.

Before closing out this section on appraisals, I want to share a more structured performance appraisal approach which focuses on competencies and values. See table 5.2.

Table 5.2 Performance appraisal of competencies and values

Performance appraisal of competencies and values		
Candidate name: _____ Role:		
Competencies for role	Individual's rating and comments (out of 5 ... with 3 not allowed)	Supervisor's rating and comments (out of 5 ... with 3 not allowed)
>	>	>
>	>	>
>	>	>
Company's values	Individual's rating and comments (out of 5 ... with 3 not allowed)	Supervisor's rating and comments (out of 5 ... with 3 not allowed)
>	>	>
>	>	>
>	>	>

This template is simple yet powerful for leaders and team members below your leadership team level, as it is directed at the competencies and skills they need to perform their roles and how well they align with the company's values. It is also easy for both the individual and the appraiser to complete. The delivery should be in a conversational manner, as with the earlier framework that I shared. It works for organisations of only 20 people as well as for those with more than 1000 employees.

Intentional mentoring of young leaders

Performance discussions and mid- or end-of-year appraisals differ from mentoring. You may choose to mentor a direct report or a high-potential leader when you see that they have significant upside and you want to help them grow, so you invest personal one-on-one time with them. However, be aware that mentoring is a significant investment for you. It is not something that you can start and stop, or regularly cancel your sessions. If you do this, it will demotivate the individual you are mentoring.

This investment in mentoring is worth it! The impact of mentoring goes beyond just the mentee; it strengthens the overall leadership capability of the organisation, and can be a motivational tool, as others aspire to be mentored by you or your leadership team.

You might think, 'I have so many responsibilities as a CEO. This is an investment of my time and a distraction from other more important responsibilities, such as time on product development or with customers'. But by investing the time to grow leaders, you create a strong succession plan, ensuring you know the leaders coming through the organisation and their capabilities. This positions the company for growth because you've identified the right leaders early. The flipside to this is you might discover through mentoring that a team member isn't ready for a leadership position. I have identified individuals to mentor and promoted them to work more closely with me, only to later realise they weren't right for the role. That can be difficult, but it is best to find this out sooner rather than later.

A simple approach to mentoring

The first step in the process is understanding whether they are open to being mentored and whether they are comfortable with you being the mentor. As the founder CEO, your offer will flatter them. They may also be nervous (remember the *leadership shadow*). Ask their permission, 'Are you interested in being mentored by me?' Some will say 'yes', and some might say 'no'. If they are not ready, do not push them. Mentoring is only effective when the individual is open and willing to be guided.

Research by Michigan State University, as quoted in Stephen Covey's book *The 7 Habits of Highly Effective People*, highlights that 50 per cent of the development journey is the person's awareness of the need to change, and 25 per cent is their desire to change. Therefore, deciding to change completes 75 per cent of the personal growth journey. Only 25 per cent involves providing them with the knowledge and skills. The individual needs to understand the importance of growth and development, and have a commitment to change.

Make it clear to the mentee that you both need to commit to this. It will be a 60-minute session each month for four to six months, depending on their progress against your agreed targeted outcomes from this mentoring.

You need to focus the mentoring discussions on competencies, values and behaviours. In your early meetings with your mentee, identify what the focus of your mentoring will be — more on this later.

Initially, you need to understand the individual, their background, and how they see themselves as a leader. The first couple of sessions are about creating a relationship with them and a sense of trust; this will occur more rapidly with you asking them questions and you listening (not speaking). Below are some example questions you could use to kick off that first mentoring session and help build your understanding of them:

- Tell me your background: why you chose your university degree, what your career is so far and what choices you have made, what your personal situation is (e.g. married, children).
- Among your roles so far in your career, which have you enjoyed the most, and why is that the case? What roles and responsibilities have you not enjoyed and why? What responsibilities motivate you the most and why?
- Who are the leaders who have influenced you and what have you observed in their leadership behaviours that you could, or that you *have*, copied? What are some negative behaviours that you have seen and why do you see these behaviours as negatives?
- Tell me some of the leadership experiences that have shaped you.
- How would you describe your leadership style today?
- What are your leadership strengths and opportunity areas? The first couple of sessions should include a discussion of any completed 360 assessments or psychometric testing.

Your role in the early sessions is to listen and to understand, not to judge or direct, just yet.

Once you understand their background, the next step, which is the most important, is to agree on what the focus area of the mentoring will be. There are three likely areas:

1. **Improvement.** Strengthening two or three of their current role competencies or leadership behaviours to increase their impact on their team, function or division, and on business outcomes. Examples could be how they can build trust and create greater accountability within their team; how they develop their own team; how to lead subject matter experts if they do not have that expertise; how they collaborate with their peers, including those

they have a conflict with; how they handle and lead in a crisis; how they lead teams that are located overseas.

2. **Preparing for a step up.** Readying them for additional responsibilities or a promotion, which may occur soon or down the track. These discussions focus on new competencies or behaviours they will need as a leader in this expanded role. Examples could be increasing their awareness of their leadership shadow (as described in Chapter 2). They will also need to learn how to lead senior leaders, as this is different to how they lead a more junior team today; how to motivate and inspire the team towards larger group goals; how to perform a strategic review on a business; and how to work with a board or investors.

3. **Personal support.** Helping them manage the stress of a new role. The first year in a leadership position is always difficult and stressful. As a mentor, you can provide guidance to help them understand and manage stress while building resilience. It could also involve work–life balance, especially if they are dealing with a major life event such as a newborn, a sick parent or a personal health issue.

Once you choose the focus area, you could use the GROW model to map a way forward. The **GROW model** is one of the most effective frameworks a mentor can use when guiding a mentee through challenges:

- **G — Goal.** What do you want to achieve? What's the bigger picture? Why is it important to you?
- **R — Reality.** Where are you now? What is your current reality? What quality resources do you have to help you?
- **O — Options.** What could you do? What options appeal to you right now? What else could you try?

- **W — Will.** What will you do? When will you do it? How will you know when you've been successful? On a scale of one to ten, how committed are you to moving ahead?

You should structure each session with the mentee in the following way.

1. General catch-up.
2. You ask, 'What would you like to talk about today? Is there an issue you would like to talk about?' This may spark a conversation.
3. Focus on one of the areas of improvement you identified in session 2.

Your responsibility as the mentor

Your role is more about listening than speaking. You have two ears and one mouth, so use them in that ratio. This may feel difficult, as you are used to being in control and directing. Your objective should be to share experiences, as opposed to telling the mentee what to do. However, occasionally giving advice is appropriate.

Know that mentoring is a journey, not a one-time conversation. As mentioned earlier, the first discussion should focus on listening, building trust, and identifying key focus areas. Holding these discussions in your office may not be ideal; meet somewhere neutral, such as a cafe or an outdoor setting. The second session should end with agreed-upon areas of development and a coherent action plan.

Meet with your mentee once a month for four to six months and then assess whether to continue or shift focus to another individual in the organisation. You can't force an individual to change or grow. If no changes are being made, then stop. This is a significant investment of your time, and if the individual is not responding, move on to someone else. Be willing to walk away if they are not engaging or applying the guidance you provide.

Founder story

Janice was leading a software as a service (SaaS) company in the US and had built her team to more than 200 people. She had a differentiated product and a passionate leadership team, although some of them had leadership gaps.

Janice knew she needed to grow her team, but did not have confidence mentoring or developing them. Consequently, she procrastinated, frequently cancelling meetings.

When I started working with her, the team told me that they appreciated her clear company vision and ability to develop detailed plans to deliver against that vision. Interestingly, they also commented that she was actually very good in guiding and developing them (which was contrary to what Janice thought). Their only complaint was the lack of time Janice spent with them, as she often cancelled or shortened these mentoring meetings.

Although Janice was good at mentoring in the eyes of her team, it was not until she began using the structured approach mentioned in this chapter that she gained more confidence and direction in how to support the team and hold these conversations. Not surprisingly with this extra confidence she did even more mentoring and she enjoyed it. Importantly, her team grew as leaders with her input.

Monday reflection

Who could you mentor on your team?

Mentoring a team member is a substantial investment and one that you cannot turn on and off. I have seen clients decide to mentor someone and then get caught up in their workload, running out of time. This can be very demotivating for the mentee. You need to stay committed.

The investment is worth it, the return on your time will be substantial, and you will enjoy it!

How to get feedback as the CEO

Recall that a disciplined leader is a *relentless student*, and this should include getting feedback on your performance from your team. You need feedback just as much as your team does.

Mostly, when a CEO asks for feedback the responses are vague: 'You're doing fine', 'I can't think of anything', or 'Leave this with me, I'll come back to you later' (but they never do). This is insufficient for your leadership growth.

Your team members will be hesitant to give feedback for several reasons. If they give positive feedback, it may seem like they are ingratiating themselves. If they give negative feedback, they fear there will be negative consequences to them. Some members of your team will have useful ideas for you, but feel unqualified to critique their boss, leading to little or no meaningful feedback.

One way to overcome this is through a structured 360-degree feedback process. This allows you to receive feedback from multiple sources, including your chairperson, board members, and direct reports. Over time, as people grow more comfortable, the feedback improves in quality and depth.

Over two and a half decades as a CEO, I rarely received feedback from my team, outside of a 360-degree approach. The only person who would give me honest feedback was the head of HR. My boss, the chairman or a global CEO would give me feedback twice a year at the formal appraisal times, but their feedback could never be as accurate as the team who worked with me every single day. Their feedback was more a KPI review, as we covered earlier in the chapter, because that's what they could evaluate. They rarely saw how my leadership behaviours were driving the business, or had insight into any of my poor leadership behaviours that may be demotivating to the team. Occasionally, a direct report might give me feedback, but often well after the event had happened. It was too big a gap, and that would frustrate me. I would think, 'If I'd only known this six months ago'. I loved feedback and did my best to respond and improve. It's immensely frustrating as a CEO to not receive feedback. No matter where you are in your career, we can all learn and improve as leaders from clear feedback on our impactful leadership behaviours.

I developed the below approach that is safe and powerful for the team to give you feedback:

1. **Prior to your next leadership team meeting, select a spokesperson.** This is to be someone you trust and who has the personal confidence to obtain feedback from the leadership team and then be able to provide you with honest feedback. It's often the HR leader, chief of staff, COO or a co-founder. Be clear to them about what you want to learn and what you're asking from the team.

2. **In your leadership team meeting, explain that you require the team's feedback to continue your growth as a leader.** Ask the spokesperson to facilitate a discussion with the team with you out of the room. Have the spokesperson ask these five questions and document the answers:

    1. What does the team appreciate about your leadership? Ideally providing examples of behaviours that are most positive and impactful.

    2. Where are you not as effective? Example areas could be: your lack of follow-up; your lack of discipline leading to meetings being late or cancelled; your lack of prioritisation of mentoring your team; your poor presentation skills; your feedback is demotivating and critical as opposed to constructive and supportive; or when you are stressed it is clear to the organisation and you are not seen as 'a person of hope' as identified as a key leadership characteristics in Chapter 1.

3. What behaviours could you change or improve as their leader to better support them? For example, stop cancelling or deferring meetings, invest one hour a month with each leader for formal mentoring and coaching, and be clearer on the strategic initiatives to drive the business towards the vision.
4. How can you more positively impact the organisation? For example, monthly all-hands meetings, a formal recognition program, better clarity and stronger reinforcement of the company's values.
5. What would they do differently if they were the CEO?

After the leadership meeting, the spokesperson considers and aggregates the feedback, which may take a few days. Their job is to identify core themes on what you are doing well and where you can improve while keeping the individual's feedback from the leadership team confidential. This can be challenging, as examples are extremely useful for you but may enable you to determine who gave the feedback ... this is a fine line to tread for the facilitator. They then sit down with you one-on-one and provide the feedback.

How you accept the feedback is critical. Be open, non-defensive and appreciative. You can inquire and try to understand more about the discussion, but do that without a focus on trying to work out who said what. Focus on better understanding the point so you can adjust your leadership behaviour.

At your next leadership team meeting, thank the group for the feedback and summarise some of the key changes you plan to make because of their feedback. Repeat this feedback gathering at least once a year. Over time, you will find the feedback gets better and clearer as the team learns to trust the process.

Another approach to grow as a founder CEO is to get a mentor or coach for yourself. More on this in Chapter 7.

Founder story

Jason was frustrated as he knew he could improve as the CEO but he never received any constructive feedback from his team. When he asked them for feedback, the answer was simply, 'You are doing a good job. Nothing comes to mind'.

He used the above approach and was amazed at the quality and quantity of feedback he received. Some of the comments he was quickly able to remedy were:

- He is a quick thinker and can be impatient, so tends to interrupt his team often, cutting them off and demotivating them from speaking up.
- They appreciate that he is busy but he is always late to meetings or cancels them, which again can demotivate the team because they prepare for these meetings.

Monday reflection

Are you getting useful feedback in your role as the leader? How can you increase that leadership feedback? By arranging a 360? Psychometric testing (such as Hogan)? Or the above approach, with feedback from your leadership team?

Monday ready

In this chapter, you've learned that as the founder CEO, your team looks towards you to develop them. They expect you to invest time with them. They respect you and want to learn from you. Over time, seeing your team develop can become one of your proudest achievements. I love this responsibility and I'm proud of the leaders I influenced in their journey. Hopefully, you'll also become that way.

Use the key takeaways list below to map your targeted changes over the first two months. Focus on only two or three changes this Monday and endeavour to repeat them frequently enough over the next month that they start to become habits. Then next month, move onto another two or three changes and again, endeavour to demonstrate them frequently.

In the next chapter, we will look at how you can be more impactful in your communication and how you can become adept at crafting and delivering your messages to influence the listeners in informal and formal settings. It is a necessary skill as a founder CEO.

Key takeaways

Develop your team's discipline.
1. Create discipline and structure in your KPI meetings.
2. Invest time in performing appraisals on your key leaders:
   - Use the 'What I appreciate' and 'How you can be more effective' approach.
   - Use the competency and values template.
3. Identify and commence mentoring a team member who has significant upward mobility.
4. Obtain feedback from your team on your performance using the framework shared.

CHAPTER 6

Communicate with impact

Even the most inspiring vision falls flat and fails to motivate the team without disciplined preparation, deliberately planned outcomes, and consistent delivery in every meeting, pitch and presentation.

As a founder CEO, you spend most of your time interacting and communicating; rarely do you work alone. Almost every moment is with your team or key external stakeholders such as customers, suppliers and investors. The smaller settings might be meetings with potential investors or prospective hires, or the hundreds of 1-on-1s you have with team members each month. The larger ones include all-hands meetings, national conferences or industry events where you may be the keynote speaker.

A key question to ask yourself is: How *disciplined* and *deliberate* am I in setting targeted outcomes for each of these interactions? Is it closer to 25 per cent? More than 80 per cent? Ideally, it should be near 100 per cent. The ability to craft and deliver your message so that it influences and moves people to your intended outcome is one of the most critical skills you must master as a leader.

Every conversation you have is an opportunity to influence, and you have hundreds of these each day. As your business scales, these conversations multiply in complexity and importance. Each meeting, whether internal or external, should have intentional outcomes. And although only a few may be formal stage presentations, disciplined preparation and delivery matter just as much in smaller settings. As a *relentless student* you should undertake regular multi-day presentation skills training as part of your leadership development. Personally, I have completed more than a dozen of these over my 30-year career, and each time I've learned something new or been reminded of the fundamentals of impactful communication.

There is substantial research that confirms why this is such an important competency for you to become skilled at, including a 2022 LinkedIn Learning report which revealed that communication consistently ranks as the top skill gap among startup founders. The reason being that early in the company's journey, identifying the product or solution that solves a customer's pain-point is the founder's most important responsibility. However, as the business scales, communication competency becomes equally essential.

Founder CEOs often see communication as secondary to technical or operational expertise in the early stages of entrepreneurship. However, from raising money to motivating your team, the quality of your communication skills is critical. Your vision may inspire, but *deliberate* communication is what secures funding, aligns teams and sustains growth.

Founder story

Kelvin had a powerful vision and a breakthrough product which was just gaining traction, so he needed funds to fuel growth. Investors were intrigued by the idea but he struggled to raise capital because his communication was inconsistent — sometimes rambling, sometimes defensive, and often unclear on the opportunity he was trying to sell.

The vision was there, but the discipline in his messaging and the structure in his communication was missing. Contrast that with another CEO who took the time to prepare obsessively for every investor pitch, considered how he could appeal to their specific fund, and fine-tuned his message accordingly. His vision was

---

understood and embraced by investors, who could clearly see and evaluate the opportunity.

The difference between these founders was not the boldness of their vision or strength of their idea or their product, but the deliberate approach to communication that brought it to life.

Monday reflection

How deliberate and structured are you in your pitches, to customers, employees and investors?

In this chapter, we cover the four essential communication skills you must master to become a powerful communicator and presenter.

1. **Learn CEO speak.** Communicate as a CEO by following essential communication principles.
2. **Be disciplined in how you hold meetings.** Structure meetings effectively to drive impact and efficiency.
3. **Learn and utilise critical presentation skills.** Master techniques that enhance your ability to influence and engage.
4. **Navigate the most challenging discussion of all, firing people and then motivating the remaining team.**

Learn CEO speak

I recall, as a young leader, sitting in meetings with CEOs and noticing that they had a unique and impactful way of communicating — one that stood out from the rest of the team. They had a capability that I call 'CEO speak'. The more I observed CEO speak, the more I noticed consistent patterns.

To improve your communication as a leader, follow these simple rules:

1. **Speak last.** It may appear strange that my first suggestion for CEO speak is to speak last. As I mentioned in Chapter 2, impactful leaders speak last. If you speak first, you set the direction, and your team is less likely to challenge or offer different perspectives, limiting the depth of discussion. Speaking last also provides you the space and time to listen actively, which leads to better decision making as you take in all perspectives.

2. **Become a skilled listener.** Don't listen to respond, listen to learn. Many people listen only to plan their rebuttal or next comment. Instead, be fully present and absorb what's being said. Don't feel you need to respond. You can thank everyone for their input and say, 'Let me reflect on this and come back with my thoughts later today or tomorrow'.

3. **Be a simplifier.** We discussed this in Chapter 2. Develop the skill of summarising and simplifying messages. As a leader, you must be able to distil complex information and then concisely communicate the issue, the root cause, and clear, actionable plans for your team. You can learn this skill through deliberate awareness in the moment as you listen to one of your team articulating an issue. Then reflect on how you can shorten, clarify and repackage what they communicated. Practise this, and over time you will improve and it will become a habit.

4. **Choose your words thoughtfully.** Maintain a positive and solution-oriented approach. Avoid overusing the word 'but' — instead, where appropriate, use 'and'. Similarly, rather than 'challenge', use 'opportunity'. Identify your communication bias with regard to 'filler' words. Everyone has filler words they overuse, such as 'like', 'you know' or 'umm'. Identify yours and minimise them because they undermine your message.

5. **Identify quotes that become shorthand for communicating key messages.** Impactful leaders use powerful quotes over and over

again to reinforce a message. They can also be shorthand for how you convey a message to your team. Find your own quotes, but some of my favourites are:

- 'Hope for the best but plan for the worst'. Being an optimist is necessary in startups but anticipate what can go wrong and be ready.
- 'Trust but verify'. I trust you but I do need to see the work.
- 'Be here now'. Be present and focused on the task or meeting that is in front of you.
- 'The more I practise the luckier I get'. The more prepared you are and the more options you create, the luckier you will likely become.

6. **Remember WIIFM (What's in it for me?)** People listen with one primary question in mind: How will this impact me? An example is your opening speech when you are new to a role and are introducing yourself to the team. The only thing people are thinking is whether you, in this role, will be good for them and the company. For example, they will be wondering whether the company grows, and whether there will be opportunities for development and promotion. When crafting any message, ensure your message connects with the audience so they hear how they will benefit, because that is what they care about.

7. **Manage emotions.** Notice I say manage emotions, not 'your' emotions. The reason for this is that in meetings individuals exhibit varying levels of emotion. Disciplined leaders are *self-aware* and are *role models,* and control their own emotions, not losing track of their key arguments or their objective for the meeting. They can also defuse situations where emotions from the other party are taking the meeting off course.

8. **Manage your own buzz.** Be your own best PR (public relations) agent without being arrogant. Avoid being overly self-deprecating. Saying things like, 'I'm not an expert, but ... ' undermines your

authority unnecessarily, and these are filler words that add no value to the conversation.

9. **Over-communicate big decisions.** As a founder CEO, you are deeply immersed in the business, but your team isn't. Research shows that people need to hear a message six or seven times before it truly sinks in. Recall the Taylor Swift analogy from Chapter 2. Although she has sung the song *Shake it off* thousands of times, she sings it with the same passion and energy every time! You must communicate your key messages with passion, energy and consistency, over and over again.

If implementing these practices feels unnatural at first, don't worry. That's normal. Over time they will become second nature. Keep this list handy and reflect regularly on how well you are applying these principles.

Founder story

Anne was the founder of a manufacturing business with a team of around 150 people. She had been CEO for six years and was immensely proud of the team and the business.

Early on in my mentoring relationship with her I assisted with a strategy retreat, and this was the first time I saw her working with her leadership team. By noon on the first day it was obvious that Anne was a very dominant leader. She would always speak first on every topic and lay out her opinions. Some of her team had the confidence to speak up and occasionally disagree, but the majority either kept quiet or simply aligned behind her views.

At lunch, I pulled Anne to one side and explained the concept of 'speaking last'. Over the next two days she endeavoured to break her habit of speaking first. She also began to proactively ask opinions from those of the team who were quiet.

A year later I again supported Anne and her team on a retreat, and this time there was a totally different atmosphere Anne would lay out the issue but then seek input from the team. The quality of the discussions this time around was far more comprehensive and collaborative than the year before, even though it was the same team.

That simple change to her communication approach of 'speaking last' had a powerful impact, providing space for her team to voice their views without being influenced by 'what the boss said'.

Monday reflection

In your team meetings are you speaking last? Do you encourage each member of your team to speak up on each issue you cover as a team?

Be deliberate in how you hold meetings

As leader, you spend a significant portion of your workday in meetings, whether it's with the leadership team, small groups or individual team members. However, many leaders fail to structure meetings with the discipline required to ensure productivity, alignment and follow-up. Every meeting is an opportunity to reinforce your leadership by driving alignment, solving problems and inspiring action. Even informal one-on-one conversations can and should have structure to maximise impact.

Why is this so important? Your time is the scarcest resource you have, so you must use it effectively. Given the time spent in meetings, you need to create a routine and approach to make them effective in moving the team and organisation towards the company's vision.

Some leaders may feel meetings are inefficient, preferring agile communication, and they dislike the structure and potential bureaucracy of meetings. They base this view on their frustrating experiences of ineffective meetings. However, a well-structured, intentional approach to meetings can address many of these concerns and demonstrate how meetings can be a powerful leadership tool.

In this section, I will explore strategies and best practices for making meetings an impactful tool in your leadership arsenal.

1. Format

The most common types of meetings for you as the leader are as follows:

- **Daily or weekly stand ups.** These meetings are a maximum of 30 minutes. You can use them for a quick update and immediate alignment with the team. Each person speaks for a maximum of five minutes and communicates their priorities for the week, and what help they may need from other members of the team to enable them to overcome hurdles.

- **One-on-one meetings.** This could be for coaching and mentoring your team, focusing on resolving a particular issue or bottleneck or alignment around the individual's or their team's performance against their KPIs and goals (as described in Chapter 3). These meetings should be a maximum of one hour — and an ideal target is 50 minutes, because it allows time between meetings to write up next steps or reset for the next meeting.

- **Leadership team meetings.** This is a meeting with your direct reports and should be held at least once a month, for anywhere between three and eight hours. Given the importance of these meetings, I will discuss them in more detail in the next section.

- **All-hands meetings.** These are for company-wide updates, culture building, and alignment and recognition. You must hold these meetings each month, normally for 30 to 60 minutes. I share more on how to maximise the benefit of these meetings below.

Offering free food is the most powerful way to ensure maximum attendance.

- **Retreats and workshops.** Retreats are incredibly powerful events to build trust and create alignment around strategic plans. If your company has more than 100 employees, you should hold retreats at least once a year for two days. Workshops could resolve specific problems or progress opportunities, such as solutioning for a major client tender.

2. Timing

Regardless of the type of meeting, be strict about the time you invest in each of these meetings and hold firm to those timings. Start on time and finish on time!

Recall that in Chapter 3 we covered the point that discipline in your meetings helps to create a culture of accountability.

3. Participants

Be deliberate in choosing the participants for the meeting and be considered in determining whether your presence is necessary. It may be acceptable for you to start the meeting, set the context and objectives, and then say to the team, 'Okay, over to you. I don't need to be here, but I would like one participant to report back to me on the decisions made'.

4. Structure

Each type of meeting must have a clear and targeted outcome. It's useful to build a standard and repeated agenda, ideally focused on three categories:

- **Inform.** What do I want to share? What do I want to learn from my team? For example, some feedback you received from investors.
- **Approve.** Are you approving something an individual or a team needs? For example, an investment.

- **Debate.** Are you discussing an issue where you're working towards a decision, or is this the start of multiple discussions. For example, early discussions on the budget.

5. Minutes

Take minutes with clear follow-up actions and deadlines, sending them out within 24 hours. These minutes are not meant to record every statement made. Instead, they're about agreeing on the next steps and identifying the actions that need to be taken and assigning responsibility to complete. I've done this for many years with my team: at the end of a meeting, I write something like, 'Hi Abhijit, great discussion today! Just confirming these are the three things you'll do, and these are the two things I'll do'. Send it out quickly, then save the message for reference, or include in the calendar invitation for the next meeting. Add deadlines to your calendar and invite the responsible people to those calendar events. This is powerful in creating accountability, as shared in Chapter 3.

Leadership team meetings

Next, I want to talk about leadership team meetings because they are critical and serve as an effective monthly tool to drive your team and the organisation forward. When determining the optimum meeting approach, seek input from your team. However, my experience is that these are your meetings as the founder CEO — so you should decide how they are run and the topics you want to address.

Understand your role in the leadership team meetings. Remember, you are on show and everything you say, do, or react to, is amplified by your position as founder CEO (recall the leadership shadow). In the meeting, being direct and disappointed is fine if something has gone wrong, but be cautious about criticising people. Don't show disrespect, or be inconsistent or unfair. As I've mentioned previously, speak last; otherwise, you minimise the debate, as the team will follow your lead.

What I've found successful in my meetings is to go around the room to make sure everyone participates when we're debating issues. There can be no passengers on your leadership team. I require everyone on my team to be an active participant and to have an opinion. Finally, at the end of the meeting, thank and recognise the team.

In terms of how these meetings should be run, it depends on the size of your business and the leadership team. If your business size is at least 100 people, I would suggest, at a minimum, plan for at least a four-hour meeting once per month, or potentially a two-hour meeting every two weeks. In smaller businesses, founders often target 60 to 90 minutes each Monday morning, and that works for them. You need to decide what works best based on where your business is in its growth journey, as well as your objectives and the need to align the leadership team.

Below are key topics you should include in a leadership team meeting:

1. Start with a confirmation of confidentiality, or agreement about what can be shared from this meeting with their teams, and what topics may need to be kept confidential.
2. Review safety statistics, if that is relevant for your business.
3. Review minutes from the last meeting and confirm progress and outstanding actions. For the outstanding actions, endeavour to lock down a date for completion. This element of the meeting assists in creating a culture of accountability.
4. Understand the details of the company's performance over the past month, so you can quickly influence forward performance.
5. Galvanise the leadership team around a short- or mid-term challenge. This might involve a tactical issue, such as addressing product issues or agreement on how to close a cash flow gap versus your budget.
6. Discuss sales and business development efforts, and how you or the team can assist.
7. Share, debate and align around functional initiatives, with each function presenting briefly on the key actions they are working on.

8. Reinforce the company's strategic direction and debate whether any changes are needed.
9. Review your HR/people plans, including staff turnover, critical hires, cultural initiatives.
10. Other business, such as an important customer visit or logistics for upcoming meetings.

In these meetings, evaluate the leadership group — both your leadership team and the level below. Bring in some of those people below the leadership team to present. This gives you a chance to observe them and evaluate their potential.

Participants should receive presentations at least three days before the meeting; presentations should be concise and limited to five pages.

Following the meeting you must complete the minutes with clear next steps, timelines and responsibilities. Some leaders have an assistant sit in the meeting to take minutes, or use AI. My preference is to complete them myself to ensure accuracy and timely distribution. If you use a different approach, ensure you check that the follow-up actions are clear with specific responsibility and timing. Your minutes should be distributed within 24 hours after the meeting.

All-hands meetings

Now, let's cover all-hands meetings. These are critical meetings and immensely powerful in motivating your team and aligning them with your vision. Remember WIIFM when communicating with the team in an all-hands meeting. Considering the audience's WIIFM is essential to engage and motive them.

In terms of the agenda, a simple structure might look like this:

1. Introduce new team members.
2. Reinforce strategic initiatives and immediate priority areas — again, use the Taylor Swift *Shake It Off* analogy. Even if

you have communicated the strategy before, the team needs to be constantly reminded, and you need to share it with energy, every time.

3. Spend five to ten minutes on a business update, such as last month's financial performance and any new customer wins.

4. Focus on one or two functional areas, having one or two of your leadership team present.

5. Discuss a new product or a customer update.

6. Recognise achievements. As shared in Chapter 3, these events are perfect for you to recognise a team member with your CEO award.

7. Have a Q&A session.

8. Provide food — people will always show up for free food! It could be a morning tea or lunch.

Why might you struggle to create and implement this structured approach to meetings? Many CEOs dislike structure, preferring an agile workspace. My suggestion is to try it out and see what works for you. You will find that this level of discipline in your meetings improves outcomes, whether the meetings are small or large. Your *role modelling* will lead your team to copy your approach with their team meetings.

Founder story

Rohit, a CEO founder of a deep-tech company in Southeast Asia, had always held leadership team meetings each week, even back when there were only six people in the company. It was a powerful routine to align the team at the start of each week.

Five years later, with a team of close to 200 people, Rohit upheld the same routine. A two-hour meeting each Monday with his leadership team to align on their activities for the week and month.

(*continued*)

He knew that he needed to evolve these meetings given the size of the team and the increased complexity of business issues. Rather than break this routine, he made two small adjustments:

1. Monday meetings were shortened to one hour, purely focused on each leader's critical imperatives for the week and where they needed assistance.
2. Monthly leadership team meetings were scheduled for six hours, following a similar agenda to that shared in the section above. This enabled deeper discussions on the range of issues and opportunities — strategic, product, customer and people.

Monday reflection

Are you deliberate in how you hold leadership team meetings? What can be improved?

Presentation skills must-haves

There is a powerful piece of research from Albert Mehrabian, a professor emeritus of psychology at UCLA, which shows that your impact and connection with an audience is 7 per cent what they hear in terms of words, 38 per cent what they hear in terms of voice tone and speed, and 55 per cent what they see in your physical presence.

Again, only 7 per cent of the impact comes from the verbal words, the literal words we say carry less weight than our emotion and energy when we speak. The way you say something — your tone, pacing and volume — accounts for 38 per cent of the impact, and 55 per cent of the impact comes from your body language and physical presence, including gestures, facial expressions, posture and movement.

When presenting to a group, consider the entire package of your presentation, not just the words you use. This is critical, because as a founder CEO, your ability to communicate effectively is one of your most powerful levers to achieve your vision.

I understand that some leaders prioritise content above all else, believing it to be the critical factor. I suggest you reflect on great presentations you've seen and recall how much of the content — the actual phrases and sentences — you remember versus the speaker's presence on stage and how they made you feel. A great quote to remember is: 'People don't remember what you say, they remember how you made them feel'. Tony Robbins, the motivational speaker, is a perfect example. He fills the stage and makes people feel energised about creating change in their lives, even though they might not recall the exact words he uses.

So, how can you take action? First, before making a presentation, ask yourself, 'What is my objective or targeted outcome?' What do I want my audience to think, feel and then do?

Once you've clarified that, determine the type of communication needed. Is it a conversation? An interactive presentation with ongoing Q&A? Or is it a formal keynote with limited interaction until the end? Choose the type of communication that will be most effective in delivering your message and enabling you to achieve your outcome.

Use the framework that follows to build your presentation and delivery.

1. Determine your compelling message

Decide on the *three* — and no more — key messages to communicate. Think about your audience's WIIFM. Use simple language and avoid acronyms or jargon.

Consider how you can validate and reinforce your key points throughout the presentation. Reinforcing key messages is a must to embed the messages in your audience's minds. People can rarely remember more than three things.

2. Plan your structure

You must start strong and grab the audience's attention from the outset. Then communicate the context and evidence or proof in the middle, and conclude with a summary that reinforces your message. Simply put, think about your presentation in three components:

1. Tell them what you plan to tell them.
2. Tell them, with evidence.
3. Tell them what you told them.

Beware of the dreaded 'boring middle' — the part where many presentations lose their audience's attention. It's crucial to keep things engaging and interactive, so your audience remembers your messages, not just how you said it. No matter how short your presentation is, there will always be a dreaded middle, so consider how to grab their attention. More on this later.

3. Start strong

This is when your audience is paying the most attention. Avoid opening with a dry agenda slide; instead, give them something memorable. For example, I started this section by sharing some statistics (7, 38 and 55%) that challenged your assumptions about the impact of non-verbal communication in presentations. The goal is to make the audience focus on your key message. I encourage you to use the phrase, 'The one thing you must remember from today's presentation is ...' This sentence lifts people's eyes off their phones and up at you, and makes them think, 'Okay, what is so important?'

4. Build credibility

Once you've engaged them, it's time to establish your credibility. Why should the audience trust you? Why are you worth listening to? What makes you an authority on the topic? The more they believe in your expertise, the more likely they are to stay engaged. Once you've set the stage, and hopefully hooked the audience to pay attention, only then proceed to your agenda — but don't let it steal the spotlight. *It's important that the audience knows what to expect, but the initial focus should remain on your message.*

5. Remember your posture

Confidence is key: stand tall, smile, and make eye contact. If you're moving around, do so with purpose. For example, walk confidently to a spot on the stage, anchor yourself and then speak your message, looking at the audience. Random wandering can distract from your message; be deliberate with your moves on stage.

Practise standing in one place with your hands by your side, looking at yourself in a mirror. You may feel awkward with this stance but when you see yourself in the mirror you realise that it looks quite natural.

6. Use clear pronunciation

Clear communication requires clarity in pronunciation. Many speakers make the mistake of delivering a punchline or joke only to drop their tone and volume at the end of the sentence, so many people miss hearing the punchline. If you're speaking to an audience, make sure everyone can hear and understand every word. *This is especially important in larger rooms or when speaking to people whose native language is different to yours.* As mentioned earlier in the CEO speak section, use words that strengthen your message, not undermine it, and use either volume or tone to emphasise key words.

7. Consider your pictures and slides

For slides, keep them simple and focused on key visuals. A great trick to test the readability of your slides is to print them out and place them on the ground. If you can't read them standing up, your audience won't be able to either. *Also, remember that less is more — less text and more impactful visuals will help people remember your message.* Focus on presenting your key ideas and let the images and charts powerfully reinforce what you are saying.

Another common mistake is cluttering slides with too much information. *Aim to keep it simple: a few powerful points, not a laundry list of details.* When in doubt, ask yourself, 'What does my audience need to walk away with from this slide?' If it's not essential to your key points, leave it out. This ensures that your slides complement your words, rather than overwhelming them.

When listing reasons, such as why a client should buy from you, limit it to three reasons. If you have a long list of reasons, your least compelling point undermines the whole list as this is what people will focus on. Choose only your three most powerful reasons.

8. Be mindful of your gestures

You need to gesture to enhance your delivery, but your gestures must be purposeful.

Use your hands, head and posture to reinforce what you're saying. Recall at the start of this chapter that 55 per cent of your impact is 'what people see'. Common gestures, including pointing, counting or even drawing in the air, can reinforce your critical points. *Slight movements* like nodding or smiling help keep the audience engaged and aligned with your message.

Keep your hand gestures and posture open and inclusive, and avoid crossing your arms, which can come across as defensive. *Be mindful of keeping your hands away from your face, as gestures in front of your mouth can distract and make it harder for the audience to hear and to understand you.* It's important to vary the size of your hand gestures to match the importance of what you're saying. Large, sweeping gestures work well when emphasising key points, while more restrained gestures can signal a shift in tone or topic.

9. Engage

To keep your audience engaged, particularly in the boring middle, use hooks. A great way to do this is by using analogies, statistics or absolutes. A statistic or analogy, like 'The average amount of water people drink in a year could fill three Olympic-sized swimming pools', will stick with people.

People remember numbers and comparisons, so grab their attention early with something that resonates. For example, instead of using the common phrase 'Our leadership team each has *five* to *ten* years of experience', why not say, 'Our collective experience *adds up to more than 100 years* of leadership'. That's something that commands attention. An example of an absolute could be a money back guarantee, or saying, 'We have never lost a client'.

The most powerful hook of all is stories! People always pay attention to stories and they can have powerful messages. Hence my personal and founder stories throughout this book.

Once you have written your presentation, reflect on what hooks you can add in to engage the audience.

10. Practise

Rehearse, rehearse, rehearse. Practise your delivery so that it feels natural and confident. I would strongly encourage you to practise enough that you can deliver the speech without notes; this is powerful as it shows that you know your content. If you need to rely on notes, try using a mind map with key points to guide you. This keeps you from reading from a script, which can feel robotic and disconnected from the audience. *Most importantly, don't obsess over a forgotten line.* The only person who knows you've missed it is you.

11. Manage your Q&A

Set expectations at the beginning of your presentation. Let your audience know if you intend to take questions during the presentation or at the end. This ensures that people won't interrupt your flow, and it lets them know when to engage. And when someone asks a question, *compliment them for their 'great question', which encourages others to ask their own questions.*

Be concise in your answers, and don't be afraid to admit if you don't have an immediate response. Politely offer to follow up after the session. *Remember, you can be like politicians if you get a difficult question. Say, 'I can't answer that question but what I can say is...' Or to reinforce your message, answer the question you wish they had asked, not necessarily the one they actually asked.*

Don't be afraid to close a question if it's not relevant to the discussion. And never be defensive — engage with confidence, not defensiveness. Finally, if you don't know the answer to a question, be honest and say so, and offer to revert to them later.

12. Hold a postmortem

After the presentation, reflect on how it went. What went well? What could have been better? *Ask someone you trust for feedback on what you did well and what you could improve next time.* Every presentation is an opportunity to learn and grow. Treat feedback as a gift and use it to refine your technique.

See my presentation skills cheat sheet in table 6.1 (overleaf).

Table 6.1 Presentations skills cheat sheet

Structure	Practise	Body language
Have a logical order: punchy introduction, middle with your main points, and a conclusion. Beware the boring middle.	Practise beforehand in front of a mirror, speaking out loud using hand movements, or in front of a peer. Practise enough times until you know it.	Smile, make eye contact, stand up straight, move around but don't aimlessly wander, walk with a purpose. Don't hide behind a podium.
Notes and handouts	**Enjoy the opportunity**	**Speech**
Brief notes on postcard-sized cards. Don't use longhand, use a mind map with key words. Provide handouts afterwards, not before, as people will stare down rather than at you.	Visualise how you will feel afterwards, when you will have done a great job!	Speak clearly, confidently and concisely. Allow gaps with breathing for the audience to catch up. Avoid jargon. Use tone. Be aware of ahhs, umms.
Visuals	**Interaction**	**Nervousness**
Keep slides clean and simple. Use pictures and charts. Don't talk to every point. Test visibility by placing it on the ground and see if you can read every word.	Build a rapport with your audience. Get them involved by asking and encouraging questions. Compliment them on good questions. Think before you answer.	It's normal, and some nervousness does help your energy level. Prepare and practise — envisioning success and breathing exercises will help.

A final thought on presentation skills. Your vision for the company is critical but it will only resonate and inspire if you are deliberate and disciplined in how you present. The above insights will assist you; however, be a *relentless student* to doing formal presentation skills training.

Restructuring the organisation and terminating staff

The last topic in this chapter is how to handle the most challenging and sensitive communication of all; restructuring the organisation and terminating staff.

You must develop this skill because the organisation will scrutinise how you manage restructuring, assessing whether it adhered to company values, and whether the process showed respect and fairness to the individuals who were terminated. The way you communicate during this process speaks volumes about your leadership — remember the *leadership shadow.*

People often comment on how well or poorly restructuring was managed. *The individuals who are 'survivors' of restructuring, the ones who stay, are sometimes just as affected as those who leave.*

A badly handled process creates a demotivated, fearful culture. The people you want to stay might choose to leave if they feel the process was mishandled. Those survivors are often your strongest employees, and it's crucial that they feel respected and secure in their roles.

So, how do you do this well?

Managing the restructuring process

1. **Start with a target outcome for your restructuring.** Is it a reduction in your expenses to increase your cash runway? Is it *the* removal of a team who has been working on an unsuccessful product and division? Is it to reduce overlapping staff following a merger? You must have a clear goal and remember the phrase, 'Hope for the best but plan for the worst'. Be aggressive in your first round of cost cutting to reduce the need to do it again.

2. **Know the detail and be involved in planning the restructuring.** This is not a task to delegate. Consider the following questions:
    *   What roles do you plan to remove and why?

- Do you have some high-calibre team members in those roles that you need to keep? Can you move them to another area?
- Are there poor performers that are not in 'redundant roles' you could remove?
- How will the terminations be implemented? When will this occur? Who will terminate the staff?
- Do the team making the terminations understand exactly what to say and the logistics of the day? Have they received speaking notes and a Q&A?
- What does the future of the organisation look like, and why is it better than the current organisation?
- Is your post restructure communication plan completed, and do all the leadership team members understand their roles in post restructure communications?
- Does the communication cover internal and external stakeholders?

3. **Be clear on the package.** When you're conducting a termination meeting with an individual *this* is critical. *Remember the acronym used a few times previously, WIIFM — What's in it for me? This* is all that they are thinking about. They may be in shock but their focus will quickly shift to their compensation. Spend limited time explaining why this restructuring is happening *because* the individual rarely cares. What they care about is the severance package. Keep the meeting brief, professional and respectful. Ideally, the employee should sign a release form to avoid future legal complications. Be sure to maintain a respectful tone throughout. They may get angry and emotional; do not lose your calmness.

4. **Try to conduct all terminations on the same day.** *The longer the process drags on, the more uncertainty it creates among the team.* Late in the week, such as *on* a Friday, is generally the best day as it provides some space for the team to understand and, hopefully, accept the change. Make sure your leadership team knows the

situation and has simple answers to all questions, as their teams will interact with them after the terminations and will want to understand more detail. *They will want to know in* particular if their jobs are still at risk.

5. **Once the terminations are done, gather the survivors.** This is your opportunity to energise those who are staying. Don't bring the terminated employees into the room for this. *Instead, focus on rebuilding momentum and reaffirming your faith in the organisation's future.* Tell the team you are sad that this has occurred. Show empathy for the departed colleagues. However, confirm that you're confident in the business going forward, while acknowledging there is still lots to do. Your job is to put the organisation back together as one team. Remember the leadership characteristic in Chapter 2; you are *a person of hope.*

6. **Following the all-hands meeting, turn your attention to focus on your most important people, your key leaders and high-potential staff.** These are the people you must keep in the business. Too often, talented people leave soon after a restructure because they do not have faith in the leader, nor in the future of the business, whereas in reality, post restructure is the perfect time for young leaders to prove themselves and achieve significant promotions. As the leader, invest your time in meeting with the high-potential team members to inspire them with the future and their opportunities in the business.

Know that an organisation's culture can bounce back quickly after restructuring if all the leaders conduct it fairly and respectfully, and if the organisation trusts its leaders.

Why might you struggle to do this? This is difficult. This is one of the hardest things that I've ever had to do in my career, and sadly, I've had to do it at least 20 times, so you need to be good at this.

Founder story

This is a situation that many founder CEOs experienced in 2022 and 2023. It was in these years that funding for many startups became extremely hard to obtain. Venture capital fund managers rapidly pivoted from a focus on a company's revenue to how quickly the company could get to cash breakeven and profitability.

Consequently, many of my clients executed significant restructuring, with some reducing their team size by 50 per cent. Almost all of those businesses are now far stronger, with more engaged teams, and are generating positive cash flow.

Why is this the case? There are three main reasons:

1. When funding was easily available many founders overspent, particularly if the spending could generate revenue.
2. There was less urgency to dismiss people who were not the right fit or were unproductive.
3. The funding shortage drove founders to focus on what was most important in the business, clear out the unproductive team members and energise the stars. This dramatically improved their businesses.

Monday reflection

Reflect on your last organisational restructure, if you have had one. What would you do differently considering the insights from the above notes on how to handle restructuring? As a CEO you are likely to manage restructures many times in your career, so document your learnings for next time.

Monday ready

Leaders leverage the power of the vision they have for their company over and over again, motivating their team to achieve great heights, inspiring investors to fund their growth, and convincing customers of the attractiveness of the company's products and services. However, *discipline beats vision*. Unless you are a powerful presenter and communicator, your vision may sound insipid and is toothless as a message. This is why, starting Monday, you need to accurately assess your ability as a communicator and make the required changes.

In this chapter you've learned that senior leaders spend the largest amount of time interacting and communicating with different groups. Being adept at crafting and delivering your message to influence the listeners in both informal and formal settings is a critical skill.

As I mentioned at the start of the chapter, I encourage all leaders to complete multi-day presentation skills at least every two years. Those statistics around the impact on audiences I shared (7%/38%/55%) reveal just how critical presentation skills are to the successful understanding of your message and vision.

I have provided a number of insights to help you be a stronger influence in your business in one-on-one meetings, leadership team meetings and all-hands meetings, and even in the toughest of them all, restructuring meetings.

Use the list of key takeaways to map your targeted changes over the first two months. Focus on making only two or three changes this Monday and endeavour to repeat them frequently enough over the next month that they start to become habits. Next month, move onto another two or three changes and again, endeavour to demonstrate them frequently.

In the next chapter, we'll explore the critical role of your support network — including your most important partner, your spouse.

Key takeaways

Communicate with impact.
1. Learn CEO speak.
   - Speak last.
   - Become a skilled listener.
   - Be a simplifier.
   - Choose your words wisely.
   - Identify impactful quotes.
   - Remember WIIFM.
   - Manage your emotions.
   - Create your own buzz.
   - Over-communicate big decisions.
   - Seek feedback.
2. Be disciplined in how you hold meetings.
   - Choose the right format.
   - Be deliberate in timing and inviting participants.
   - Choose the right meeting structure.
   - Complete and circulate minutes promptly.
3. Build your presentation skills.
   - Compelling message.
   - Clear structure.
   - Start strong.
   - Solid posture and move with purpose.
   - Clarity in pronunciation.
   - Powerful pictures and slides.
   - Complementary gesturing.
   - Engaging the audience.
   - No notes, know what you plan to say.
   - Practise, practise, practise.
   - Hold Q&A.
   - Perform a postmortem.

4. Handle tough conversations effectively. Navigate the most challenging discussions, including firing people and motivating the remaining team.
   - Have a target outcome.
   - Be clear and fair on exit packages.
   - Ensure the LT know their roles.
   - Develop a Q&A pack.
   - Plan deliberate timing for terminations.
   - Hold a follow-up all-hands meeting, including WIIFM for survivors.
   - Engage and retain high-potential survivors.

CHAPTER 7

Build your support team

Becoming an outstanding leader is not a solo journey. You must be *deliberate* in designing the support team that will encourage you, hold you accountable, and educate and train you as a leader.

Think of top tennis players. The best in the world do not rely on vision and talent alone. They have the discipline to assemble a team that keeps them physically, mentally and emotionally at their peak. The best players have a comprehensive team to support them on their journey. They will have a technical coach — often the person you see in the players' box — and they'll also have:

- a conditioner to help build their strength and endurance
- a nutritionist to advise them on their diet
- a physiotherapist to help with injuries or to provide massages after the game to relieve tight muscles
- a sports psychologist to ensure they are mentally in the right space to be at the top
- an agent or business manager to assist with endorsements and sponsorships
- a financial manager to provide financial advice and help them manage their winnings and endorsements; and
- a life (intimate) partner, sibling or parent who is always present in the players' box for emotional support during the game, and who can offer friendship and camaraderie afterwards.

As a founder CEO, you need the same *deliberate* approach. You must decide who belongs in your 'players' box' today and reassess that regularly as your business scales and your life circumstances evolve. The right support team is not static; it will grow, contract and change over time. What matters is that you build it intentionally.

In this chapter, we will cover:

- How to make your life partner your partner.
- How to find other supporting members or partners to have on your side.
- Why you should consider a coach or mentor, and how you can find the right one.

Make your life partner your true partner

You know the importance of investing time, energy and resources into self-development, and of building trust and accountability with your teams in the business. But do you place the same level of importance on your most critical and hopefully longest relationship — your life partner?

They are likely to be in your life much longer than this business. Are you seeing this relationship as a two-way street, supporting your partner on their own journey as much as they support you? Being a founder CEO is a seven-day-a-week job. Have you had a conversation with your partner where they agree to accept that imbalance for periods of time? And more importantly, have you had a conversation about how to rebalance things when the business is not in crisis mode?

I know the importance of a successful relationship with your life partner through my experience with my wife, Melinda. I could not have achieved the same career or financial success without Melinda by my side for over 40 years. We've worked well together to raise three amazing daughters — Sophie, Emily and Paige — who are all now in their thirties, married, having children and achieving success in their own careers. As with any relationship, it takes ongoing commitment to make this work.

Melinda and I have had considerable challenges to navigate during my 25-year CEO career, including a total of 11 country moves and 29 house moves. We have been fortunate to have had great mentors and role models who have helped us to understand and recognise the importance of making your life partner your partner.

I have another story for you — but first, recall that a disciplined leader is a role model for your team in how you lead the business. Your relationship is another of those examples where being a role model is a powerful motivator for those who are watching you.

Booz Allen was a top-tier consulting firm in the mix with McKinsey, BCG and Bain. It was purchased by PriceWaterhouseCoopers (PwC) in 2014. I loved my time at Booz Allen; I was there for six years, built strong relationships with my colleagues, and enjoyed the work thoroughly. After six years, they promoted me to principal; a role that is theoretically undertaken one or two years before a partnership would be offered. However, I left Booz Allen because I looked at the partners and in my opinion saw few healthy long-term relationships. Most partners worked extremely long hours with little control over their lives, as they were always on call for clients. Many partners were divorced, and some of them multiple times. Maybe I was wrong in blaming the work for their divorces, but I could not see enough role models at the partner level to encourage me and inspire me to stay.

Although this is one of the last few topics in the book, it is arguably the most important. You are likely to be in a relationship today. Maybe you're married and have young children. I'm certain you are time-poor, with many demands on your time. However, you can be both an impactful leader and a supportive partner, but as with so many of the topics we have covered in the book, it takes a *deliberate* approach.

Alternatively, you may think, 'I'm not in a relationship today. The most important thing in my life is the startup I'm creating'. This may be the case, but it will change. If it doesn't change, you may find yourself financially successful but very alone.

Approaches to building a true life partnership

First, read through this list yourself and consider the suggestions. Then read it with your partner and discuss it to learn what resonates with them.

1. **Communication is key.** Open and honest communication with your partner instils a feeling of trust and security. Listen, intending to learn and not to fix. As CEOs, we often jump in and try to fix issues with advice on what our partner should do. Ask your partner whether it's okay for you to give an opinion or advice. They may say no. We're used to problem solving but that may not be what your partner wants or needs. Holding back and simply listening may be the most valuable support you can provide.

   To broach difficult topics, use the approach of clearing the air. Say, 'I'd like to clear the air. Something you said made me feel like this'. Your feelings are undeniable. This is a sound base to build a discussion from. It may feel clunky at first but over time it can become a natural way for you both to clear issues or frustration in the relationship.

   If you feel there's tension, there probably is. Remember, one of the impactful leadership characteristics I shared in Chapter 2 was 'Trust your gut'. Don't shy away from the simple question, 'What's wrong?' Melinda and I endeavour not to go to bed when there's tension and any potential anger, although it's generally me who speaks up. I will say, 'What's the matter? What have I done wrong?' My favourite approach to reduce tension is to apologise, saying, 'I'm sorry for what I did', but secretly I may be trying to figure out my mistake. The apology is often the first step from which you can rebuild.

2. **Choose your battles.** Neither of you will always be right, and not every discussion needs to end up with you being right. Determine

whether the argument is worth your energy; if not, simply say, 'That's fine with me', even if your competitive nature wants to continue debating.

3. **Turn towards each other.** During hard conversations and tough times, turn towards each other, not away. When it's a tough conversation, sometimes the tendency is to think this is too hard and walk away. Turn towards each other physically and say, 'Okay, we need to resolve this'.

4. **Agree and communicate the non-negotiables.** Perhaps this could be your Friday date night, reconnecting every week or two. Maybe it's children's events you must attend. Maybe it's exercise time for both of you. What are your non-negotiables? Be clear and hold firm on the agreement.

5. **Involve your partner in understanding your business vision but don't make them part of the stress.** I've always spoken about my business challenges and successes with Melinda, and she has been an intelligent and unbiased sounding board for me.

6. **Make time for each other.** The easiest ways are date nights a few times a month, or a regular Sunday morning walk together. Although you are spending time together, you may not be connecting as it is easy to fall into a conversational routine, such as only discussing your kids or your aging parents or work challenges. To mix things up and connect on new topics, agree not to talk about family and work. Sometimes, it's good to have them as veto topics. Sometimes on our date nights, Melinda and I play backgammon — the best of three. We also try to come up with three different questions to spark a discussion that isn't about family or work. This keeps our conversations fresh, and more like they were when we were dating.

7. **Celebrate.** Be your partner's number one cheerleader, not their critic. Be the one to hold them up and show appreciation. Reflect on whether, and how often, you are doing this. Remember also

that minor acts of appreciation—like a handwritten note, or a simple 'I'm proud of you' at the right moment—go a long way in strengthening the bond. As an example, sometimes when I am travelling I open my bag and find brief notes in there from Melinda encouraging me or saying how proud of me she is.

These behaviours might differ from how you've approached relationships in the past, so focus on the areas that feel most natural to you today.

Founder story

Brian's tech startup was booming. Clients were lining up in Singapore, Australia and the US. However, he only had a small team of 12 so he was literally working 18 hours a day, seven days a week. Although the hours were long, the opportunity was massive and he loved what he was doing. Janice, his wife of two years, was not as happy.

After one of our sessions, Brian made some changes that had an immediate impact on his relationship:

1. He involved Janice more in discussions about what was happening in the business. As a result, she felt more connected to his journey and was also able to add value, with an often clearer view by not living in the day-to-day of the business.
2. He instituted date nights every second Friday where they reconnected on topics outside of family and business.
3. They agreed the non-negotiables; specifically what events Janice needed him to attend or support. She accepted how hard he worked and so kept her requests minimal and therefore achievable for Brian.

Monday reflection

How are you staying connected with your partner? Is it time to institute date nights every couple of weeks?

Why you need a network

Just as a strong personal relationship creates a foundation for success, your professional network plays an equally critical role in your growth as a leader. Think back to the example of the tennis player and the team that supports them. You also need a team to help you achieve your vision for the company and balance in life. At different times your needs will change, and this team will also need to change.

Recall that disciplined leaders are *relentless students*. Building a support network is one of the most powerful ways for you to accelerate your learning or fill in your knowledge gaps. Running a startup requires expertise in product development, hiring, funding, legal, operations and marketing, and the list goes on. No single founder excels in all of these, particularly early in their careers. By surrounding yourself with experts in these areas you can make better decisions and scale more efficiently.

Networks shortcut the learning curve, helping founder CEOs avoid costly mistakes. Talking to people about what they've done previously, and what has worked for them, can help you accelerate your own learnings significantly. Investors also have a bias towards founders who are proactive in building networks and seeking advice from people who have done it before.

Often the best hires come from referrals. Without a network you may limit your ability to find exceptional talent. People prefer to work with leaders they trust, and a strong network can build your credibility.

Networks can also speed up product adoption and customer acquisition by making use of your advisors' network. This may be through identifying new and different ways to test or pilot your product, or by introducing you to a customer who is open to trial your product because they trust the judgement of the advisor who connected you.

If you think you don't need a strong network, ask yourself, 'Do I personally know how to solve every challenge my company will face?' If the answer is no, and it always is, then you will know that investing time in building a strong network is essential. The strongest leaders recognise that learning from others is a competitive advantage.

How to build a network

The points below will help you to be deliberate and disciplined in building a network that complements your skills.

1. **Be methodical in your planning.** Analyse your existing network and deliberately decide how to improve it. Much like you desire diversity in your business, target diversity in your network. This could be gender, age, nationality, geography, political persuasion and, most importantly, expertise in an area in which you are weak. Actively seek mentors and peers who challenge your thinking rather than just those who affirm it. These people could be from your industry, an adjacent industry, academia, government or regulators.

2. **Be diligent in your tracking.** Transfer your contacts into a spreadsheet or database with a name, company and role. Analyse this and identify who you should reconnect with. At this stage you rarely know who may, or may not, be able to assist you on your journey. Don't hesitate to contact those you haven't spoken to recently. Your reconnection may flatter them, and they're unlikely to judge you. However, acknowledge the time gap with a comment like, 'Long time no speak, but I thought of you and would love to reconnect, if you have time'.

3. **Be comfortable and confident, reaching out to softer connections.** A softer contact may be someone you met briefly at an event. Reach out and say, 'We met briefly. I'd like to connect

and learn more about your business /experience /company /etc.' Rarely will the person say no.

4. **Have a plan for the meeting.** Be clear on what you want to achieve or learn from the meeting. It may be to gain an insight into their industry, to learn more about their background, or to gather insights and suggestions from them on specific issues you are facing. Before each meeting, take five minutes to research their background so you can ask insightful questions to start the discussion.

   You may be nervous about how to handle this meeting. My learning is that people *love* to talk about themselves. If you have five questions to start, then you have nothing to worry about regarding kicking off a productive conversation.

5. **Make each meeting multiplicative.** In the meeting, notice how you may reciprocate and help them with an introduction. At the end of each meeting ask, 'Who else would you suggest I speak with so I can learn more about this topic? Would you mind introducing me over email or WhatsApp?' The connection from them to that person significantly increases the probability that this new person will meet with you.

   If you're connecting people to other people, take the time to write a nice paragraph about each of them with generous wording. It helps them but could also assist you down the track as it sets an example of how they can introduce you to others. At the end of the meeting, thank them profusely for their support. Your reputation as a connector will enhance your credibility and make people more willing to help you in return. The more value you bring to others, the stronger your network becomes.

As busy leaders, networking is something that can stop, as you just don't have the time. My suggestion is: *make the time.* You will definitely get a return from this investment — it is just that it will likely pop up as a surprise.

Why you need an advisory board

When your business is small a single mentor might be sufficient, but as your business grows, build an advisory board. It is well worth your time. You will benefit from:

- **Targeted expertise.** You can bring in advisors with the exact industry or functional experience you need, whether it's for the next six months or a few years.
- **Focused problem solving.** Advisors can help you tackle specific challenges, such as fundraising, navigating regulation or entering new markets.
- **Strategic access.** The right advisors can open doors to key customers, partners and investors through their networks.

You may wonder why people would want to be on an advisory board. Not surprisingly, many experienced people would prefer to be on an advisory board and not have the legal obligations of a formal board position.

You may be concerned about what to pay them as you have limited funds, but advisory board members don't need to be paid in cash. Many people will join an advisory to support you, or out of an interest in the business you're creating. Occasionally, you may offer shares as compensation.

You may believe you're too busy and don't see an ROI in building an advisory board. But to be a *relentless student* you should surround yourself with a strong support system. Your network and advisory board will give you a significant ROI if you build it *deliberately*.

Start small when building an advisory board — say two or three people with complementary experience to each other — and meet a couple of times a year as a group. You do not want this group and the meetings to become a burden for you. This group must add value through their experiences and assistance.

Founder story

Marvin had a formal board, however, he felt he needed deeper insights from experts in other areas.

He decided to build an advisory board and structured it in the following way to provide him the insights he needed without adding bureaucracy and lots more meetings to facilitate:

1. Marvin recruited three advisory board members who had very different skills to his existing board, including deep expertise in his areas of interest.
2. He arranged for quarterly calls with each individual member to guide and mentor him.
3. He set up only two, formal, two-hour meetings a year, at which all three advisors were to be present.
4. In each formal board meeting, which were held every two months, he put in a 15-minute agenda item to update the board on his insights or actions as a consequence of input from the advisory board.

Monday reflection

Is it time to set up an advisory board? If so, what is the best approach to allow you to receive insights without creating extra work for yourself?

Get a coach or a mentor

The last piece in the puzzle to support you is using a coach, mentor or advisor. This can often be the same person. I am more of a mentor and advisor to my clients, but I use coaching skills and reflective questioning in discussions to prompt deeper insights.

Let me explain the difference between a coach, mentor and advisor.

A **coach** helps you think and grow through self-discovery. They're focused on using structured frameworks and asking powerful reflective questions. A coach will rarely, if ever, give advice. For example, a leadership coach helps the CEO refine their decision-making process through guided reflection. The right coach pushes you to explore your assumptions, recognise blind spots, and build a leadership approach that is uniquely suited to your strengths and challenges.

A **mentor** also uses reflective questions but shares more personal experiences and insights to help a leader navigate challenges. They provide wisdom, encouragement and perspective based on their own careers and experience. The mentor sessions are often discussions covering immediate issues that the mentee is dealing with. An example is a seasoned CEO mentoring a founder on handling a difficult employee, or an investor relations issue, offering specific stories from their own experiences to help the founder make informed decisions.

An **advisor** provides direct expertise and recommendations to help leaders make more informed decisions. Typically they're a subject matter expert or former executive, and are engaged for specific issues or business challenges, such as enterprise selling approaches, fundraising and market entry. They're more directive and solution-oriented than a coach or a mentor. Examples are a financial advisor guiding a CEO on capital markets and options to raise money, or a sales expert using their deep expertise to educate the leader on B2B sales techniques.

I'm a trained and accredited coach but work as a mentor and advisor with clients in the startup community in Asia, India, the Middle East and Australia. My clients employ me based on my experience as a long-term CEO, my Impactful Leadership framework (much of which I've shared here in this book), and my experience working with around 150 founder CEOs. These experiences allow me to bring not just a structured approach, but also real-world insights that help founders make better strategic and tactical choices.

All founder CEOs benefit from having a coach, mentor and advisor in their corner, supporting them on the journey to create a successful business while also helping them with their personal wellbeing. I've been fortunate to have had amazing mentors, each possessing skills that complemented my personal growth at various career stages. These relationships added something unique, from leadership wisdom to crisis management skills, and helped shape the way I approach my leadership and mentoring today.

Most successful entrepreneurs have coaches. One of the most famous is Bill Campbell, who coached some of the most successful technology leaders early in their journeys, including Steve Jobs, Eric Schmidt, Jeff Bezos and Mark Zuckerberg. I would suggest you read the book *The Trillion Dollar Coach: The Leadership Handbook of Silicon Valley's Bill Campbell* to learn more. Salesforce CEO Marc Benioff credits Tony Robbins and other mentors for shaping his leadership. If these world-class CEOs relied on coaches, why wouldn't you want one as a founder CEO? They recognised that having an external perspective and structured guidance allowed them to accelerate their growth and navigate the complexities of leadership more effectively.

Leadership is a skill that must be honed continuously; you need to be a *relentless student* of leadership. Even if you feel confident in your abilities, blind spots exist. A great mentor or coach can reveal these areas, challenge your assumptions, and push you towards better decision making.

Independent of significantly successful CEOs having coaches, there is considerable research that confirms this. In 2021, *Harvard Business Review* reported that 71% of executives improved team performance with coaching. McKinsey, in 2021, found that startups with founders who had external coaching, advisory, or mentoring support were three times more likely to scale successfully. My clients can also validate the benefit of having a mentor in their relationship. Visit my website for the testimonials (www.impactfulleadership.com). These statistics and real-world experiences illustrate the tangible benefits of having structured support in place.

It is lonely as a CEO: there are few people you can talk to. Many people have a vested interest in you, or they have a vested interest in your outcomes, such as the valuation of your company. However, coaches and mentors only focus on supporting you to make the right decisions *for you*. Their role is to create the space for you to explore and refine your leadership approach and life journey in a way that aligns with your vision and values.

You might think, 'I don't need a coach. I can figure it out myself'. Even Olympic athletes, who are the best in the world, have coaches. Why? Because they are *relentless students*, knowing they need to keep learning and improving, because their competition is doing just that. They know that by talking to someone with expertise they can improve their performance. Leadership is no different.

You also might think it's too expensive for you. It is expensive, but if coaching helps you make a better decision or avoid a poor decision that costs you thousands of dollars, it's a great ROI. The best leaders don't see coaching as a cost; they see it as an investment in their own personal growth and the success of their business.

Maybe you're thinking, 'I don't have the time for coaching'. A good coach helps you make faster and better decisions, so it will help you free up time. Several clients have said, 'I'd love to use you. I just don't have the three hours a month'. My response is always, 'My goal is to assist you to find more time by short-cutting your learning by using my experience'. Investing in coaching and mentoring is about prioritising informed decision making and long-term success over short-term 'busyness'.

You might say, 'My board and investors already give me advice'. Your investors have their own agenda, and that agenda may not be right for you. A coach and mentor work solely in your corner and have your best interests at heart, helping you manage stress and make better decisions.

The best CEOs recognise that leadership is not a solo sport. They build a support system around them of trusted advisors, experienced mentors and expert coaches to ensure they are constantly improving.

How to find a coach or mentor

The following is a structured approach to determining the type and style of coach or mentor that best aligns with your needs:

1. **Define what you need help with.** It may not be easy for you to know your gaps but try using the evaluation you completed in Chapter 1. The gaps are typically in knowing your role as CEO, building trust and accountability with your team, industry understanding, functional expertise, working with boards and fundraising. There is a wide spectrum of what your gaps may be so it is important for you to consider what they may be prior to finding a coach.

2. **Decide what type of support you need.** A coach or mentor who's done a lot of this before, or an advisor for a specific issue. Do you want narrow support, or wider guidance that helps you problem-solve as you scale?

3. **Make sure you're committed to doing this.** It is an investment in dollars and will take your time. As I mentioned, I require three hours a month — two sessions of 90 minutes for a minimum of six months. But most of my clients go on for over 12 months, and I've worked with some of my clients for four years.

4. **Source potential coaches and mentors.** Leverage your network. Start with the investors, advisors and fellow founders. They often know experienced mentors and coaches. Reach out to ex-bosses, former colleagues and industry leaders you admire. Attend founder events and industry confidence groups to meet potential mentors. Engage on platforms where mentors are active, such as LinkedIn, and search for potential mentors and coaches. Listen to podcasts and webinars where potential mentors share insights.

5. **Investigate through lots of conversations.** You now know what you want. When speaking with potential mentors, you can see how they line up. First, consider your 'fit' with them by investigating the following areas:

   - Is there alignment with your goals and values?
   - Does the coach have experience and a structured approach (such as my Impactful Leadership framework) that aligns with what you want to achieve?
   - Do they specialise in the areas you need help with, such as leadership development, scaling a business, or managing investors?
   - Is there chemistry in their communication style?
   - Do you feel comfortable, open, and potentially vulnerable with them?
   - Do they listen, or over-speak?

   If you have a trial session, consider:

   - Do they challenge your thinking in a way that helps you grow?
   - Are their questions leading to self-reflection?
   - Are they providing the type of support that you want? Coaching or mentoring or advising?
   - Do they help you translate insights into real actions and outcomes?
   - Do you think they can hold you accountable without being overly rigid and prescriptive in what they're doing?

   The key here is understanding whether they meet your needs in terms of what you want to achieve, the relevance of their experience, and the fit.

6. **Confirm their track record and capability.** Have they successfully coached or mentored other founder CEOs or leaders in similar industries or situations? Do they have the testimonies and recommendations from people you respect? Ask to talk to their previous clients to understand how they work.

How to be a good mentee

From your side, you need to be a good mentee. This requires you to:

- **Be present** and focused in the sessions.
- **Commit and endeavour not to cancel or change.** Most mentors can be a little flexible. However, you may end up paying for sessions because of your cancellation.
- **Bring issues to the session.** I want my clients to come to sessions with at least two business issues they're facing. Being a founder CEO, I'm certain you'll have at least two issues to talk about each session.
- **Follow up.** Take notes, reflect on the discussion, and follow-up after you've had the session. This could be further self-reflection of your leadership behaviours or specific action on a topic covered, such as having a conversation with one of your leadership team who is missing their commitments (recall the concept of 'consequence' in Chapter 3).
- **Know when it's time to move on** and feel comfortable stepping away. Down the track, you may re-engage with the same mentor or someone else that better suits your needs as you've changed over that time.

The two biggest barriers for having a coach or mentor are cost and your time. With the right person you will get a tremendous return on that investment.

Monday ready

In this chapter, you've learned how to be disciplined in how to recruit and work with a team that can assist you on your journey. Stop thinking that you can do it on your own. You need a support team to help you as a leader. Make your life partner a true partner. Build an advisory team and get a coach or a mentor.

People join you on your journey for a reason or a season, and some join you for a lifetime. Be deliberate in who you recruit in each of these areas!

Use the key takeaways list below to map your targeted changes over the next month. Focus on only two or three changes this Monday and endeavour to repeat them frequently enough over the next month that they start to become habits. Next month, move onto another two or three changes and again endeavour to demonstrate them frequently.

In the next chapter, I will share with you my thoughts on the number one mentoring topic with my clients: working with boards. The board members' responsibility to the investors far outweighs their responsibility to you. As a founder CEO, you must take charge of the relationship and the interactions with your board. If you do not, then they will.

Key takeaways

Build your support team.
1. Make your life partner your true partner.
   - Communication is key.
   - Choose your battles.
   - Turn towards each other.
   - Agree the non-negotiables.
   - Involve your partner in understanding your vision.
   - Make time for each other.
   - Focus on 'we' rather than 'me'.
   - Be your biggest cheerleader.

2. You need a network and multiple partners.
   - Be methodical in your planning.
   - Be diligent in your tracking.
   - Be comfortable and confident, reaching out to softer connections.
   - Have a plan for the meeting.
   - Make each meeting multiplicative.
3. Build an advisory board.
4. Get a coach or a mentor.
   - Define what you need help with.
   - Decide what type of support you need — a coach, a mentor who's done a lot of this before, or an advisor for a specific issue.
   - Make sure you're committed to doing this.
   - Source potential coaches and mentors by leveraging your network.
   - Investigate through lots of conversations.
   - Confirm their track record and capability.
5. Be a good mentee.
   - Be present and focused in the sessions.
   - Commit and endeavour not to cancel or change.
   - Bring issues to the session.
   - Follow up.
   - Know when it's time to move on.

CHAPTER 8

Lead the board — don't be led by it

The board members are not your best friends. Their responsibility to investors far outweighs any responsibility to you. Many factors govern that responsibility, including their fiduciary duties if the investment is coming from a fund, as well as corporate law, which dictates their legal obligations. It has little to do with how they feel about you or whether they like you.

A great shock often faced by my clients is realising that passion and vision alone will not secure the board's support — that support will only be achieved through deliberate execution, transparency and results. Misunderstanding the board's priorities is one of the biggest risks to founder CEOs and can threaten the success of your business. In this chapter, I'm going to explain how you can mitigate that risk.

I've been a director of startups, public companies and philanthropic organisations. I've also been a chairman of multiple companies, and I've been a CEO of a publicly listed entity in Australia. So I have been on both sides of the boardroom table, as a board member and as a CEO, and each side has significant challenges. These experiences have also reinforced my view that boards have far more respect for disciplined leaders who deliver than they do for visionary ones who don't — even though they may admire the vision.

Without a doubt, the biggest challenge all my founder CEO clients face is learning how to work with boards. Again, *you need to remember that the board members are not your best friends.* The board is answerable to investors and contributors to its fund, and your job is not to just try to win it over with big-picture thinking. You need to consistently demonstrate that you are in control of the business and that you do what you say you will do.

As CEO, you must build a relationship with the board and take charge of your interactions with it. If you don't, the board may take charge of your company's direction, which could be at odds with your vision. The worst-case scenario is that you lose the board's confidence and, ultimately, your own job as CEO — even if you are the founder and a significant shareholder. I have seen this happen a few times.

In this chapter, we will focus on three topics:

1. The shocking truth about the board's priorities.
2. Guidance on how you can take charge of board meetings.
3. The optimal board meeting template to use in future meetings.

The shocking truth about the board's priorities

Founder CEOs often have a critical blind spot in understanding their board, and this misunderstanding can be the main reason for losing control of their company, access to investment or even their own job.

Some of the key themes for you to keep in mind are as follows.

1. **The chairperson and the board will support you every day publicly until the day they fire you.** What I mean by that is the board needs to be outwardly supportive of you as the leader. This visible support provides reassurance to investors and the wider public. However, at some point, and sometimes very quickly, the board may lose patience in your ability to drive the business or become concerned about your lack of transparency. This could rapidly lead to your exit, even if you are a significant shareholder.

2. **The board members' top priority is risk mitigation to protect their own reputations.** Board members are deeply concerned with how a company's failure could negatively affect their own professional reputations. Board members are very proud of the companies they represent. However, if things go wrong and a company fails or publicly faces major issues, their reputations will be directly affected. Therefore, protecting their reputations is almost always their number one priority. This is a surprise to almost all my clients, because this is not how they think.

3. **The board's second priority is fiduciary responsibility to its shareholders or fund contributors.** For example, a VC fund has investors who have placed money into the fund. The fund then assigns board members to your company and those board members have a legal, fiduciary responsibility to the investors who invested in the fund. Similarly, if the board is part of a philanthropic organisation, it is accountable to the fund's contributors. These fiduciary duties are significant obligations.

4. **Business performance is often the board's third priority.** This surprises my clients the most. Despite what most founders believe, risk mitigation and fiduciary responsibility take precedence over business performance. This is surprising, because business performance is the CEO's number one priority, by a long way.

5. **Lack of transparency is your greatest risk to staying CEO.** The next surprise for most of my clients is that your *lack of transparency* with the board is likely the greatest risk to your reputation, your relationship with the board, and your employment. The board considers this more important than the business performance itself because lack of transparency by the CEO puts points two and three (above) at risk. You may think that you are being transparent in your decision making. However, if you do not provide the board with context for your decisions, it will fill in the gaps with its own interpretation, which could be completely wrong.

For example, you might have decided to exit a major customer, break off the partnership with a co-founder, or fire a senior leader in your company who has the board's respect. You need to provide the context for these significant decisions. This context will help the board understand the reasoning behind your choices.

The reason I say that lack of transparency is such a significant risk to you is that if you're a CEO performing below expectations, you'll likely have a grace period of six months, a year, or even 18 months before the board loses patience. Conversely, a lack of transparency, withholding information, or misleading the board could cause your immediate dismissal (even if you are a significant shareholder). That's why transparency is such a high-stakes factor in your relationship with the board.

6. **Remind them.** Another important thing to keep in mind is to remind the board members of what you have told them previously. You need to remind them regularly of the points previously discussed, as they may have forgotten the details or the context of your prior conversations. Board members in VC funds could serve on 20 or 30 boards at once. It's not unreasonable for them to forget the detail of a conversation you had with them two months ago. Be clear and consistent in your board papers before meetings and during one-on-one conversations to remind them of what you said you would do, and what you've done.

Another reason you need to re-communicate key messages is that you understand the business better than anyone else. You understand every detail of your business because you're involved in it 24/7. Board members, on the other hand, have no involvement in the day-to-day operations. They engage based on your outreach or scheduled board meetings. It's important to know that when you explain concepts or decisions related to the business, you may need to over-explain them. They might not grasp the level of detail you know intuitively, so provide extra clarity when necessary.

It's easy to underestimate the board's power and influence. In the early stages, investors will woo you, especially if your product or service appears to have significant potential. But once a crisis hits, the board's behaviour may change dramatically.

Ultimately, you have no choice but to form a productive relationship with the board. Like all the topics covered so far in this book, there are *deliberate* actions and behaviours you can implement to build a strong, impactful alliance with the board.

Building a productive relationship with the board

Follow the below steps to build a productive relationship with your board.

Step one: Agree with the board your mutual responsibilities

Here's what I know works best. Your board's top three responsibilities to you are:

1. **Set a direction** for you and your team, or confirm your plans.
2. **Support you,** particularly in overcoming bottlenecks, or using their network to assist you.
3. **Mentor and advise you,** and likely key members of your team, leveraging the board members' extensive experience.

Your top three responsibilities to your board are:

1. **Respect the board members' position, their legal responsibilities and goals.** This is fundamental. The board is there for a reason, and understanding its role in governance, ensuring legal compliance, and recognising its goals and priorities is crucial. You must respect the responsibility board members bear to investors, their legal obligations as directors, and their goals of an attractive financial return. An example of how this can be challenging to accept is you may receive a

buy-out offer and want to reject as it is too low. However, the board may need a liquidity event for its fund, so push you to accept the offer.

2. **Be transparent.** Transparency is key. Keeping the board informed, not just when things are going well but especially when things are tough, builds trust. Avoid the temptation to hide problems; the board is there to help you through the tough times and the good ones. And remember that if you do not provide context, the board will create its own — which may or may not be correct.

3. **Be 100 per cent accountable for your responsibilities and what you told them you would do.** When you make a promise or set an expectation, you must deliver on it. Remember in Chapter 2 we discussed how creating a culture of accountability starts with you role modelling that behaviour to the team and the board.

Step two: Build rapport and a strong relationship with the board

Building rapport and trust with your board members is essential for a successful working relationship. It's a long-term investment in your leadership and their perception of your ability to lead. Start by investing time to understand each board member individually. What is their background? Why are they on your board? What are their priorities? Board members have varied focuses and interests — What are their individual 'hot buttons'? Some board members may be extremely product-focused while others may be revenue-driven, often asking questions like, 'What is your top line revenue and the growth rate?' Still others may only be concerned about monthly cash flow and the burn rate, asking 'How much cash do we have in the bank? How long is our runway?' Understanding each board member's priorities is critical. The better you understand these concerns in advance, the better equipped you'll be to address them in meetings and have a more productive discussion, as opposed to being sidetracked by a board member deep-diving into their personal area of interest.

Arrange regular one-on-one meetings with the chairperson, ideally fortnightly or monthly, depending on their availability and interests. Establishing this relationship with your chair is essential for creating alignment before board meetings. You should also set up quarterly one-on-ones with other board members. While not as frequent, these meetings allow you to cultivate personal relationships beyond the formal board setting. Come prepared with an agenda for these one-on-ones. Use these sessions as 'show-and-tell' opportunities where you can go deeper into certain topics than you might not share in a board meeting. This can allow individual focus on their 'hot button'. In these meetings be clear about what feedback, input or help you need. This makes them feel valued, and can increase their engagement and alignment with your vision for the company.

It is important to build a relationship with all the directors. However, remember that the chair has the most responsibility in terms of leadership on the board. Building a strong relationship with them is especially vital, as they can help you influence the other board members and be a key partner in navigating strategic or controversial decisions.

Step three: Be comfortable asking the board for help

As a founder CEO, you must leverage the resources and expertise of your board. Be comfortable asking them for connections, advice and support for solving problems.

One of the biggest areas of support is introductions from board members to their network. This could include connections to senior leaders in companies that could be potential customers, or into potential suppliers where you may receive favourable pricing which you may not have received without the board members' help. A final area here could be in identifying potential employees the board members may know.

They can also provide specific help in board meetings. If you are expecting pushback in a board meeting, use one of the board members to be an advocate for your proposal, especially if you expect some resistance from other members. It's not uncommon for board members to have differing opinions, so having one or two board members 'in your corner' can help rally support when you need it.

You can also ask specific board members to assist with mentoring key members of your team. For instance, if one of your directors is a former CFO and your current CFO has development needs, ask for advice or help. Board members often bring deep experience in specific areas that can benefit your team, so use their expertise to lift the skills of your team.

Founder story

Charlotte was leading a fintech business that had performed strongly over the five-year period since launch. Early on, the board consisted of just two investors and Charlotte, but given the recent series B raise, the board had expanded to four representatives from different VC funds and herself.

The board meetings occurred every second month and Charlotte was comfortable with the content covered and the interactions with the board. Her only frustration was that she expected much more from the board members, beyond their contributions in the meeting.

Often they would offer to help with potential customer introductions, but these never eventuated. There was no follow-through on their part.

In my discussions with Charlotte, we identified what she needed to do differently:

1. Put these commitments into the minutes of the meeting, being specific about which board member would contact which potential customer, and by what date.
2. Charlotte put a note in her calendar two weeks and four weeks after the board meeting to follow up with the board members responsible for introduction.

These two changes were effective in ensuring her board members did what they had committed to.

Monday reflection

Are you leveraging your board's connections? Are your board members doing what they promise? If not, what can you do to increase their accountability?

Step four: Be confident asking them to leave

Many founder CEOs are also the chair of the board. Personally, I do not think this is ideal as having an independent chair can add tremendous value and learning for you, and it is also what most VC funds would expect if they were investing, from series B onwards.

If you are both the CEO and chair, you need to be extremely thoughtful about building your board. When recruiting a board member, ask yourself, 'Am I comfortable firing them if they don't work out?' This is never a straightforward question, particularly if the person is someone you trust or have close ties with. It is critical to be honest with yourself about the effectiveness of each board member. If they are not adding value, are not fulfilling their responsibilities or are causing conflict, it will only harm the company in the long run. Don't shy away from tough decisions, which can even mean firing a board member who was a close friend of yours when they joined.

Many founder CEOs struggle with board dynamics because of their lack of confidence, especially when dealing with older, more experienced, and often strong-willed individuals. After all, these board members are representing the investors and have significant experience in managing businesses and expectations. However, as the CEO, this is an area where you must step up and deliberately take control.

If you cannot take charge of the board, it will quickly take charge, and this can create significant headaches. The sooner you take control of the situation, the sooner you'll feel more confident. Over time, as you practise managing your board and gain experience in handling the diverse personalities of the board members, your confidence will grow. This process is often the most challenging part of the startup journey, particularly for first-time founders, but it is entirely manageable using the above *deliberate* approach.

Manage the board meetings

Board meetings are critical touchpoints for your relationship with the board, and though they may be infrequent for early-stage companies, they are significant. They can either build or undermine your reputation with the board. That's why it's vital to control the meetings' structure, content and flow.

Each board meeting is career day. You are on show. Don't underestimate its importance. Make sure the board documents are correct and you know the content, in that you can confidently address every element of the pack and answer questions with authority. You cannot afford to be surprised. You must know everything in that board pack and cannot blame your team for any mistakes in the documents.

I've been on boards where the CEO said, 'Oh, actually I didn't know that we put that in'. Or 'Oh, I disagree with that. My CFO must have put that in'. That sounds terrible and undermines your credibility with the board. You must know and understand everything in the board pack. If you're not across it, it will raise doubts in the board's mind about your competence and leadership.

When I was at Booz Allen as a consultant, I remember a partner said to me one day, 'Dane, every time you open your mouth, you gain or lose market share'. That's the same with board meetings. Every time there's a board meeting, the board will evaluate you and you will either rise in terms of their respect or you will decline. These evaluations aren't just theoretical, they have real consequences. For example, these meetings can impact the investors on the board in whether they do follow-on investments in subsequent rounds. These are important days, even if they are only two hours long.

Most founder CEOs are product or technical experts, and may not understand financial accounting. In that situation, ensure that your finance leader also attends the board meeting so that he or she can respond to questions that may be too technical for you. With that said, learning finances and accounting is very achievable. I'm an engineer, and I was a CFO for close to 10 years. The learning curve might be steep at first, but accounting principles are well within your grasp as a *relentless student*. Once you master the basics of financials, you will feel much more empowered during these discussions.

In the meeting itself you need to take charge. If there's a vacuum, board members will fill it, and that often leads to discussions that are off-topic and unproductive. This lack of direction and control in the board meeting can erode their confidence in you. When they sense a lack of decisiveness or clarity on your part, they may view it as a sign of weakness, which is a direct threat to both your leadership and potentially the company's success as the board may become directive and push the business in the wrong direction.

Founder story

Calvin constantly struggled with his board as its frequent requests for information overwhelmed him. This was exaggerated by his failure to understand why the information was needed.

An experienced board member requested very specific financial data, but Calvin, lacking a financial background, didn't understand the request's purpose. My role was to educate him on why the board needed this information and to help him craft a board agenda that met both his and the board's needs.

Over time he became more confident in managing board meetings. He also started providing both the detailed financial data requested and the insights he felt board members needed to understand the business and the reasons behind his decisions. Thereby he enhanced his credibility.

Monday reflection

Are you managing your board meetings, or are the board members? How will you change this dynamic? The first step is to be deliberate in your agenda and hold firm to it.

Some founders might see limited value in their board members beyond the capital they bring to the table, and may view board meetings as an obligatory exercise to their investors. My perspective is that board members are experienced and can offer significant value beyond their financial contributions. They bring broader perspectives, insights, connections and strategic guidance to the table.

That said, board members need to be managed. If you don't direct them, they may end up contributing little to nothing to the company's success.

By proactively managing your board, you can maximise their value and minimise the likelihood of them becoming bureaucratic obstacles.

How to frame your board meetings

Listed below are my top tips for a productive board meeting.

1. You must own the agenda and lead the meeting

A focused, well-led board meeting, driven by the critical issues, is powerful. Your ability to direct the conversation and ensure everyone stays on topic and focused on the critical issues will contribute to your company's success. Once you take control of board meetings with a clear agenda and pre-meetings for alignment, you set the tone for a successful, less stressful meeting. Over time, this becomes more intuitive and you will feel less anxious going into these sessions.

2. Establish regular pre-meetings with the chair and key board members

Ideally these would be held seven days before the board meeting. This will allow you to prepare the chair and key board members, forewarn them about any critical issues, and provide context for the discussions.

Remember that board members are often involved on multiple boards and may not have the time to read every detail of your board pack. This is another reason the pre-meeting is useful. In the pre-board meeting be succinct and remind them of important points from previous meetings, any changes in the business or surprising insights that have been identified since the last meeting, what you want to achieve at the upcoming meeting, and where you may need their assistance.

3. Know each board member's hot buttons

As we discussed earlier, certain board members are more focused on the quality of your team, others may be focused on the revenue, while some will look to cash flow or operational issues. Ideally, aim to connect and resolve any potential issues with board members prior to the board meeting. If that is not possible, tailor your board pack and meeting presentation to address these hot buttons first to prevent them from derailing the discussion.

Even if you do this, a board member still might take control and move the discussion in an unproductive direction or dominate the meeting with a discussion that is only about their hot button. It's okay to say to them, 'That's a good point, but given our time constraint in this meeting, can I have that discussion with you after the board meeting or at another time?' It's your job to keep the meeting focused and ensure that the conversation stays on course.

4. Be clear about your goals for the meeting

Know what you want to achieve — whether that's agreement on financial forecasts for an upcoming fundraising round, approval of the next year's budget, or securing support for a team remuneration package. Whatever it is, ensure your board pack supports these goals and don't hesitate to push for decisions in the meeting.

5. Be deliberate in what is, and what is not, included in your board pack

Many founders make the mistake of overloading their board with excessive information. For example, I've seen board packs for startups with annualised revenue of less than US$5 million stretch to over 200 pages. That's simply too long. Even for publicly listed companies this level of detail may not be necessary. You need to focus on the issues that matter and create a concise yet informative pack that facilitates decision making. Don't inundate your board with details that distract from the key issues at hand.

An overcomplicated board pack only serves to dilute the focus of the meeting and slows down decision making. Instead, structure the pack around the tactical and strategic issues that are most important for the company's success. See the next section of the chapter for an example board template.

Ensure that you send the board presentation to the board at least a week in advance to increase the probability that they will review it. This gives them ample time to go through the materials thoroughly, which leads to more productive discussions. Be ready for the board responding to you on a Saturday or Sunday with questions prior to the meeting. Initially, you need to respond to those questions. You should address issues promptly and explain things clearly and concisely. Over time, you need the board to understand that your team works very hard as it is, and spending the weekend responding to board queries is probably not the best use of your team's time and energy. You need to work through that. Of course, at times you will need to scramble because you need to respect the board's questions but it is important not to let the board take too much of your team's time for queries that can wait until after the meeting.

6. Assign tasks to the board members

Remember, the board has a responsibility to support you in the business. Give them tasks to complete, such as an introduction to a potential customer or investor. Ensure this is minuted and that you follow up (as shared in the earlier Founder story).

7. Thank them

At the end of the board meeting, thank them, regardless of how the meeting went. This might be hard, especially when you're feeling frustrated or dissatisfied, but it's important to remain professional and gracious.

Founder story

Rachel wanted to pivot their product because their existing product had a very long sales cycle, putting pressure on the company's cash flow. The founder CEO and the team had developed another similar product, but with a shorter sales cycle.

She was, however, extremely worried about how the board members would react to this pivot because they saw significant potential with the existing product, although they were frustrated by the slow sales.

Rachel realised that explaining and winning over the board could not be done in a board meeting so she arranged multiple sessions with individual board members, showing them the new product and the early traction that it was receiving.

By the time the board meeting occurred, all the directors enthusiastically supported the pivot. It is unlikely they would have been as supportive if this were a surprise topic at the board meeting.

Monday reflection

How disciplined are you in setting the board meetings up for success through prior discussions and education of the board on major issues?

I appreciate that the above may initially feel overwhelming given the experience and dominant nature of some board members. If that is the case, my suggestion is to identify a board member who can assist you in controlling other board meetings or navigating some of the more controversial issues. Find someone within the board whose leadership style aligns with yours and who will be comfortable, at times, being a strong advocate for you in meetings with more challenging topics.

Finally, step up and own the board meeting. I appreciate it's a lot of effort; however, if you use this disciplined approach, it will pay off. You will build your leadership credibility while guiding the board towards becoming a real asset for your company.

Create a board template

A standard board template helps you, as the founder CEO, in several different ways — from preparation to ensuring that focus stays on the right issues. Specifically, the benefits of the consistent template are:

- It saves you preparation time each month and each quarter with your board meetings.
- It is a powerful way to focus the board and meeting discussions on the levers that drive business growth and profitability.
- It trains the board regarding what to expect to see each board meeting. It also shows the trends in the business, providing the board with clear insights and information about opportunity areas.

The feedback I receive from the board members of my clients has been that this has helped them. They appreciate the consistency of the papers, and also that the document covers the most important areas for them.

You do not need to follow the template in table 8.1 exactly. Add or subtract pages that are most relevant in your business and use this template as a foundation.

Table 8.1 Agenda template

AGENDA
1. Minutes from prior meetings and follow-up
2. YTD results and outlook
3. Sales performance
4. Major strategic and tactical initiatives
5. Assistance requested
6. Back-up (not planned to be discussed, unless specific questions)

1. **Minutes and follow-up.** This covers the action points that you agreed at the last board meeting or at prior board meetings.
2. **Year-to-date results and follow-up.** This is your financial performance. If your board meetings are monthly, it is the prior month; if your board meetings are quarterly, it is the prior quarter. It includes:
   1. year-to-date numbers versus budget or versus forecast
   2. an outlook for the balance of year
   3. your full-year expectation — is it still on track with a budget? In this section, you also might provide information on gap-closing plans. If it looks like you're behind budget, what initiatives will you implement to close the gap?
3. **Sales performance and business development initiatives.** Sales performance could be new contracts or expansion of work with existing clients. It includes opportunities, and major clients you're going for if it's an enterprise business. This section includes tracking and sharing the performance of your sales team versus their targets. Things like organic growth and any price increases you put through are important. It could also include major strategic clients where you need assistance or introductions. The template in table 8.2 is useful, particularly for B2B companies tracking major contract opportunities.

Table 8.2 Sales and business development template

Initial discussions	Tender stage	Tenders submitted and presentations planned	In negotiation
Total Potential Units = Total Potential Rev =	Total Potential Units = Total Potential Rev =	Total Potential Units = Total Potential Rev =	Total Potential Units = Total Potential Rev =

4. **Major strategic and tactical initiatives.** This could be an update on your major strategic initiatives, for example, tactical changes associated with the product; or a discussion about new recruits you've brought in or insights about people that you've lost. There are a number of different areas you can cover in this strategic and tactical section.

5. **Assistance you want from the board.** This might be a check on the status of a previous request to the board. It is also where you raise other requests, such as a request to a board member who has the requisite status and presence to help in negotiations with a large client. (One of my clients brought in their chairperson several times during final negotiations with big enterprise clients because that enterprise client wanted to see some grey hair, and this helped my client to win those contracts.)

6. **Back-up.** This could be show-and-tell with your product; examples of marketing, and additional financial information such as balance sheets you didn't need to show in the main pack.

What might stop you from doing this? Well, number one would be board members pushing their own template that aligns with their other portfolio companies. You need to respect that. But what you may do is put those pages in your back-up. You need to keep your board pack to less than ten pages. You will not get through any more than that, I promise. It's vital to keep it concise and focused around the updates you need to share, the decisions that need to be made, and the help you expect from the board.

Founder story

Rowena had three different VC funds invested in her business and each had a seat on the board. Unfortunately, two of these board members had their own requests on what they wanted to see in the board pack. (It is not uncommon for investors to impose their own framework for board packs, often due to their fund requiring reporting on certain KPIs that they feel are critical.)

To resolve this challenge while also keeping the board pack focused on what she felt was critical for discussion, Rowena met with each board member and discussed the below three options to ensure the board pack met their objectives while also being a catalyst for important decisions:

1. Provide the requested information in a separate pack to the directors prior to the board meeting.
2. Include the requested information in the appendix of the board pack.
3. Agree with the board which pages need to be discussed in the board meeting and which can be into the appendix.

Monday reflection

Is your current board pack helping you achieve your objectives in the board meeting? Can it be improved?

Monday ready

What you've learned in this chapter is that the board members are not your best friends. Their responsibility to their investors far outweighs their responsibility to you. Your biggest risk is lack of transparency. Give them context. Otherwise, they'll create their own. As a CEO, you must take charge of the relationship and interactions with the board. If not, the board will.

What must you start doing? Be disciplined in investing a lot of time in building rapport with the board, and in preparation of the board papers. Keep the key themes of working with a board top of mind, including your efforts to build rapport and relationships. Use the proposed approach I've shared with you to hold board meetings and use the board meeting template.

Use the list of key takeaways below to map your targeted changes over the first two months. Focus on only two or three changes this Monday and endeavour to repeat them frequently enough over the next month that they start to become habits. Next month, move onto another two or three changes and again endeavour to demonstrate them frequently.

In the next chapter I will show you how to go global — the holy grail for every startup and the essential step towards international success and a valuation in line with your vision and investors aspiration.

Key takeaways

Lead the board, don't be led by it.
1. Be aware of the board member's priorities and responsibilities.
   - They will support you publicly every day, until they don't.
   - Their #1 priority is risk mitigation.
   - Their #2 is fiduciary responsibility to their investors.
   - Their #3 is the business's performance.
   - Your lack of transparency is your greatest risk.

- The board's responsibilities to you are to confirm the company's direction, support you to overcome bottlenecks, and mentor you or members of your team.
2. Be aware of your responsibilities to the board.
   - Respect their position and responsibilities.
   - Be transparent.
   - Be 100% accountable for what you say you will do.
3. Build rapport and a strong relationship with the board.
   - Meet regularly with the Chair and the board members.
   - Understand each person's hot buttons.
4. Control the board meeting.
   - Own the agenda and lead the meeting.
   - Be clear on your objectives for the meeting.
   - Hold pre-meetings with the chair and key members to align on major controversial issues prior.
   - Know each board member's hot buttons and be prepared.
   - Use the board template to create a focused board pack.
   - Assign responsibilities to the board members; leverage them and hold them accountable.
   - Thank them at the end, even if you don't feel that way.

CHAPTER 9

Grow internationally through proven global approaches

U nless you're a US-based company, you must expand internationally. You will never achieve the valuation you aspire to unless you do so. Expanding into international markets is exciting for many reasons.

1. Your product or service is performing well in your local market, so you logically expect success in similar markets.
2. International markets offer significant potential and the chance to multiply your existing revenue and profit.
3. Your leadership team, board, and investors have confidence in your expansion plans and the forecasted returns.

Leaders often massively underestimate the path to success in international markets. As business leaders, our optimism is mostly a strength as a vision of a sizeable international business motivates the team for overseas opportunities, and investors for a stellar return. However, our optimism can also be a curse when we underestimate the risks and distractions, and the disciplined leadership required to enter a new market. Risks, at a minimum, include:

1. Customers and consumers can appear similar across markets, but generally, they are more different than alike.
2. The business model in your local market may not be appropriate for the new market, creating complexity as you endeavour to operate in a manner that you have limited experience in.

3. It's easy to overlook how tough the competition is; they'll have strong customer ties and may not follow local regulations or laws as closely as you do. They might see the greyness in some of those laws or they simply ignore them. Whereas you know you need to be fully compliant, if not, your investors will have a problem.

4. Your current team does not have the time to support an international market when things go wrong, which I guarantee they will. And when I say the international team, I mean you as well.

5. The time to become cash flow positive is at least two or three times longer than forecast.

I know these issues very well as I led multi-country operations for over 25 years, including launching Taco Bell as a new brand in Australia and having a front-row seat to the exponential growth of KFC China in the 2000s.

Let me share these stories which have different endings, one happy and one sad.

Taco Bell: A test case

As mentioned earlier, I was with Yum! Brands, the global owner of KFC, Pizza Hut and Taco Bell, for about 12 years. One of my responsibilities in the late nineties was launching Taco Bell in Australia.

Taco Bell is one of the top-performing quick-service restaurant brands in the US, and having lived there for almost ten years, it was my favourite as well. The food offering is tasty and varied, and it's a very strong and well-recognised brand. At Yum! Brands, we believed Taco Bell would be hugely successful in Australia given that our market research confirmed consumer excitement about the brand. We also looked at supermarket sales of similar products — such as Old El Paso, which sells the ingredients for customers to make their own tacos, burritos and quesadas. It was one of the fastest-growing supermarket categories for over a decade, and it is a huge category even today.

With those factors in mind and, given the many cultural similarities between Australians and Americans, I was very confident about Taco Bell in Australia. We opened 15 stores over a three-year period. Then, about eight years later, when I was the International CFO based in Dallas, I remember signing a capex to close all 15 stores. We had lost about US$30 million over those eight years.

So why did it fail? We attributed it to three key factors:

1. When you walk into a KFC, McDonald's or Pizza Hut, you know exactly what you're getting: pizza, burgers or fried chicken. But with Taco Bell, the menu confused people. There is a lot of variety and it takes people a few visits to identify their favourite product. We suspect many customers came in a few times and could not find a product that resonated with them.
2. Success in fast food and quick-service restaurants depends on attracting the 'cool' 15- to 20-year-old crowd. Even with TV marketing and advertising we couldn't make that happen. We could not connect with the right demographic and encourage them to come back as frequently as the passionate users did in the US.
3. This last one surprised me: We had strong operations with KFC and Pizza Hut in Australia, but we really struggled with Taco Bell. The consistency and quality of our food at that time were not up to the standard they were in the US.

Unfortunately, the launch of Taco Bell in Australia was not a success. This is a clear case of vision without discipline. The brand, research and excitement gave us confidence but we lacked the disciplined localisation, operational consistency, and consumer understanding needed for success. Our inspiring vision alone was not enough.

(Interestingly, Taco Bell did a relaunch in Queensland in November of 2017 and as of September 2025 had grown to 37 stores.)

KFC China: Discipline turns vision into success

Now let's look at a good news story, KFC China. I was the International CFO for Yum! Brands between 2002 and 2006, with responsibility for finance, supply chain, store growth, M&A and IT in all markets outside of the US. China, therefore, was one of my responsibilities and so I visited that market around 30 times over a four-year period.

Under the leadership of Sam Su, the then China CEO, the team built a phenomenal brand. They had a deep understanding of consumer differences between China, the US and other markets, tailoring both the menu and dining experience to local preferences. In the US, the menu included around 29 items, while in China the menu was over 50 items. The Chinese consumer loved variety, so on their plate they would have six to eight different items, including tea, spicy chicken, fish or shrimp product, chips, rice, gravy, local salad, a local delicacy of some sort, and a dessert such as a custard tart. KFC in China also held more aspirational value than in the US. As a result, the restaurants were much larger — while a typical US KFC had 30–40 seats, some locations in China had 300 seats. This shift in positioning proved highly successful.

Another critical element was the standard of operations in China which was arguably the best in the Yum! Brands global portfolio. This superior operation enabled the company to launch 50 new products a year in limited time offers, where the US only did five to ten. This drove repeat business, with customers coming more frequently to experience the variety while also receiving consistent, outstanding service quality.

There is a Harvard Business Review case study from November 2011 that does a wonderful job of explaining the KFC China success story. I would recommend this to any founder CEO planning to expand overseas, no matter what your industry.

When considering your own business and the potential for international expansion, you may challenge the idea that international expansion will be difficult. Maybe you believe your product or service is universally appealing and not significantly affected by cultural, economic or regional differences. Perhaps you think, 'Success at home proves success abroad'. Or maybe you feel confident that your operational capabilities will allow you to overcome challenges in new markets. My answer to that? Consumers and markets are different. Hopefully the above stories on Taco Bell in Australia and KFC in China prove that point.

You may be thinking that the above examples relate to traditional, manufactured or service-based industries but your product is a digital solution solving corporate or consumer pain-points. From my experience mentoring deep-tech and SaaS founders across Asia, the challenges are remarkably similar:

1. **Customer realities differ.** Overseas users may interact with technology differently, prioritise different features, or operate with different digital habits. What delights users in say, Singapore, may be difficult to seamlessly offer to customers in say, Vietnam or India. Localisation isn't just getting the language right, it's understanding workflow, integration norms and buyer psychology.

2. **Digital ecosystems vary wildly.** Cloud infrastructure, app stores, payment gateways, and even data-hosting preferences differ by country. Security expectations and procurement processes can also vary dramatically. Navigating these inconsistencies requires the same discipline you'd apply to a complex supply chain.

3. **Government and regulatory frameworks shift rapidly.** Digital and data laws, particularly in Asia, can change overnight. Consider China's tightening data rules or India's evolving digital governance; both can quickly alter the playing field for international SaaS providers.

4. **Local partnerships can make or break expansion.** In deep-tech, partnerships with telcos, cloud platforms or government-linked entities often define whether you scale fast or stall entirely.

Choosing partners carefully, with clear governance and mutual trust, is crucial, but is not easy to do. Many companies progress through at least a couple of partnerships over a number of years before finding the right partner.

Over time, I've found that difficulty in leading businesses rises tenfold when you have international operations. Leaders often underestimate the difficulty of expanding into new international markets and do not foresee the number of things that inevitably go wrong. You may also take your eyes off your local market, which suddenly starts to plateau because you now need to invest time and focus on these new markets.

Regardless of the challenge, expanding overseas is necessary. If you're in Southeast Asia, success in one market will not be a large enough value driver for your company. A compelling and exciting vision will inspire the team and investors, but knowing how to scale with leadership discipline in international markets is a critical skill you need to develop as a CEO.

This chapter will provide approaches to achieving success overseas, including:

- Understand the two key business drivers: the market (your target customers/consumers), and the business dynamics of other countries.
- How to find the right leaders and develop trusting relationships.
- How to build a culture, consistent with your local operation, and how to ensure compliance.

Understanding the market and the business dynamics

First, on the market and your target customers; it's a lot tougher to win over customers than you might think in international markets, even in countries that seem similar. Customers behave differently, even in comparable countries, and even words in the same language can have completely different meanings. One example is the 'sloppy joe'. In Australia, a sloppy joe is a sweater or pullover. In the US, it's a sandwich with meat and lots of sauce. Even within countries there can be significant variation. For an example, look at India; people in southern India generally prefer spicy food, while those in the north prefer less spice. China has similar differences in their taste preferences across the country. Also, as mentioned above, in the digital space customers may have similar pain-points but may be more difficult to target or connect with due to the local digital ecosystem.

Business dynamics and models may need to vary from your local model. For example, you may have a direct sales force in your country, but in a new market you may decide that using a distributor is the fastest and lowest cost approach to generating revenue across the country. Going down this path if you have never used a distributor before can be extremely challenging. Your own sales force focuses only on your products, and you can direct and control them in real-time. A distributor may be selling hundreds of other products, so getting their focus onto your product can be slow and challenging. And if they are not gaining sales traction, they are more likely to blame your product rather than their sales force. Many companies change distributors multiple times before finding the right one to drive their product.

Founder story

Phuong was the founder CEO of an HR tech startup which was the market leader and powering ahead in its local market of Vietnam. The product was an HR information management system and payroll service, including rostering, time and attendance, and pay calculation. The solution her company offered was relevant to every market worldwide, so she was confident about the opportunity as she expanded in Indonesia.

(continued)

However, after three years of effort she decided to walk away from that market, for a few reasons:

1. Her solution was very good but local companies were not prepared to pay the 25 per cent premium for her product, compared to inferior local solutions.
2. Her growth in Vietnam had slowed as her team spent considerable time in Indonesia endeavouring to support sales efforts, and extensive time customising solutions for any work that they did win.
3. Indonesia was cash flow negative for the three years, with no clear line of sight as to when that would change.
4. Her board lost patience and encouraged her to refocus on Vietnam, thereby increasing the business as an attractive acquisition for similar companies wanting to break into Vietnam.

Monday reflection

Have you experienced similar challenges when you have entered a new international market? If so, are you clear on what you would do differently in your next expansion move?

Customer focus

How can you, as the leader, navigate international expansion successfully? Consider these key areas:

- **Clarify your value proposition and have a clear point of difference.** Do this before entering a market and be prepared to refine it continuously over the first 24 months. Tom Sant, the global marketing expert and author, created the NOSE principle as a framework to create a powerful value proposition. Let me explain it simply here:

- **N** stands for **Need.** What is the customer's need that you are targeting to satisfy? Another way to think about this is, what is the customer's pain-point or their key problem that needs resolving?
- **O** stands for **Outcome.** What is the outcome or result that the customer desires? As an example, this could be a product benefit or cost saving.
- **S** stands for **Solution.** What solution are you offering to clients that satisfies their **Need** and delivers the **Outcome** they desire? How does your product or service work to resolve their pain-point? This may be unique to them or could be a generic solution that solves the problem for large or small groups of customers.
- **E** is for **Evidence.** What evidence does your company have confirming that your solutions work and deliver the outcomes customers want? You need to prove to the customer that your solution works and that you have done this many times before.

Using the NOSE principle is an insightful yet succinct way to build your value proposition. Your initial plan may not work in this new market, so you'll need to test and improve your product and its value proposition several times before finding the right fit. In my experience this can take 12 to 36 months, depending on the speed and breadth with which you can test your product or offering.

- **Be selective with your product range or service offering.** Start with a focused offering and adjust for local preferences. Success in one market doesn't guarantee success in another, so adopt a **pilot approach**. What does that mean? Instead of launching at scale, test with just a few locations. If you're expanding a food chain or retail stores, for example, open two or three outlets in a regional city rather than launching 10–20 stores. If your product is software, again, start with a small offering so you can analyse acceptance and use of the product. Learn what works before you scale; it will help you maximise the impact of your most important resources (cash, people, time and your focus).

- **Expand city by city, not across the whole country.** Cultural differences can vary widely within a country. Build success in one city, or region of a city, before moving to the next. Earlier I used the example of taste preferences differing across regions in India; preferences also change in food, clothing, music, sport, etc. To maximise your product or service's appeal, investigate regional differences across the country and concentrate your marketing efforts on the most receptive city or town.

- **Know the local competition.** They'll be tougher to compete with than you expect. Some may not comply with labour laws, giving them a cost advantage. Competing in second- and third-tier cities can be especially difficult, as local businesses often have deep-rooted customer relationships. When entering a country, do a thorough analysis of the advantages the competitors may have over your business. Take off your rose-coloured glasses when you are doing this evaluation. Too often I have seen the founders be too optimistic about competing with local competitors. Remember the optimism trap mentioned earlier; we can look for the positives and avoid seeing the underlying negative data. Evaluate the competitors with a critical eye.

- **Local country leaders.** When dealing with enterprise customers, local leaders have substantial decision-making power. Just because a global CEO in the US, or a regional CEO in Singapore, endorses your product doesn't mean local teams in other countries will automatically sign on. In fact, sometimes it's the opposite, as they prefer the local suppliers and companies they already have relationships with, or who are bribing them to use their products (more on that later).

- **Prepare for complex meetings.** In India, China and Southeast Asia, there may be 20 people in the room, but only one decision-maker. Do your research to identify who the key person is and focus on winning that individual over.
- **Scrutinise customer contracts.** Omitting key terms like price regulation and change-of-law provisions in B2B deals can quickly turn a profitable deal into a loss. Many markets also include unfavourable clauses like uncapped liability and consequential loss, which you should reject. However, understand that this could put you at a disadvantage versus local competitors, as they will probably accept these clauses. The reason being they have multiple companies to protect their total business from substantial claims, or they are comfortable taking the risk as it is a limited liability company.

Business model and cost structure

When entering a new country, equally important to finding product-market-fit is building the foundation for the business to deliver excellent service at the lowest possible cost. Below are some key areas for you to investigate:

- **Identify all potential cost levers, early.** In most businesses, regardless of the service or product, the highest cost item is labour. Before you enter the country do your research on how to minimise these costs. For example, labour costs, including social benefits, can vary significantly by city no matter which country you enter. In China, for example, social benefits can add up to 40 per cent on top of base wages, but this differs by 10 to 15 per cent between cities like Beijing, Shanghai and Shenzhen.

    The evaluation of cost levers should be exhaustive prior to your launch to best position your product financially from the outset. The below framework is useful in considering sourcing strategies in new (and existing markets) based on the volume of raw material or service that you purchase, and its criticality to the delivery of your product or service (see figure 9.1).

VOLUME	**HIGH**	Aggressive price reduction with one supplier	Multiple suppliers with comprehensive contracts
	LOW	Lowest cost sourcing	Single supplier with multiple contingency plans
		LOW	**HIGH**
		CRITICALITY	

Figure 9.1 Cost levers framework

- **Plan for supplier and distribution failures.** Issues arise all the time in international markets. The discovery of a carcinogenic colouring in a spice mix created a major crisis and serious business disruption for KFC China in 2004. Be thorough in your early evaluation of suppliers. This review must be broader than simply cost. For example:
  - What is your sourcing strategy for each key item? For example, a single supplier or multiple supplier approach?
  - For each supplier, who are their largest customers and what is their reputation in the market?
  - Do they have robust quality assurance programs?
  - What contingency plans exist in their business?
  - Do they have adequate insurance cover if things go wrong?
  - What are your contingency plans for each of your offerings?

- **Protect your brand.** Social media can destroy credibility in an instant. Monitor online sentiment closely and have a strong PR strategy and crisis-response plan ready.
- **Expect to spend significant time in the market.** You and your leadership team will need to visit at least once a month in the first two years. It may seem excessive, but being on the ground is critical to evaluate the attractiveness of your product, understand real-time challenges, build direct customer relationships and evaluate your team.
- **Plan for a longer road to cash flow positivity.** This always takes longer than forecast. Keep the mindset: *Hope for the best, plan for the worst.*

To overcome the challenges mentioned above, know that an expansion plan falls heavily on the CEO, so you need to have the time to focus on this country. You must also find an outstanding team to lead that business. Which brings us onto the next topic of how to find and work with outstanding leaders.

Importance of finding the right overseas leader

Initially, you may place one of your team into the new market. However, for the greatest long-term success, you will require a talented local leader. In every country there are disciplined and impactful leaders. If you are not a local it is difficult to find them, and costly when you make errors, which I can guarantee will happen. For example, when you make an error in recruitment, that person may end up running the business in a totally contrary way to your values, or worse still, you may have a fraudulent experience with them as leader. Although planning your recruiting approach reduces the risk of making errors, the risk always remains.

Regarding my own experience of finding leaders in new countries — it has always taken me longer to find them than I expected, and I have made many mistakes.

Let me share a story. I once had regional responsibility for a business overseas and had to let the country manager go for inappropriate actions. More on that later in the chapter. It then took six months to find a new CEO who I thought looked strong on paper and he interviewed well. However, once he was in the role, he never seemed to complete what he said he would do. He also struggled with one of the concepts I mentioned in Chapter 2 — that is, going from 10 000 feet, then into the detail and back up to 10 000 feet. He got stuck in the detail and couldn't get himself out. He did not have the strategic mindset that the business needed, so we both decided he should leave the business.

Given the challenge of finding a leader and the insecurity it was creating for the local team and customers, I stepped in as the interim CEO for around 14 months while also doing my regional CEO role. It took us that long to find the next leader.

The point of my story is that outstanding leaders exist in all markets but it's hard to find them and expensive if you don't — in terms of actual expenses and, even more importantly, your time. An example of the expense for me was my 'double-hatting' — doing the country manager role and my regional CEO role — and I'm sure there were things I missed in my regional role because I was focusing on the country where I was interim CEO. Also, you need local leaders to lead local teams because they understand the customers and market better than you do.

Instead of recruiting local talent, you may think you can delegate this opportunity to your team. My answer to that is, yes, your team can certainly play a critical role in this new market. However, it's unlikely they will understand the nuances that exist in a new market with new customers, and your ongoing success in your own market requires the focus of your local team. You don't want them to be distracted by issues in this new market.

Founder story

Ming led a deep-tech business that had expanded into six Southeast Asia markets, each of which, he felt, offered material revenue upside. His local market was Singapore where he had a team of over 100 people, including 30 engineers, and where they had the biggest enterprise contracts. Given his strength in product development, he spent most of his time working with the engineers. He also was very close to the large Singapore customers and was effectively the account manager for them.

This meant he spent very little time in the seven other markets. Without his focus, almost all of them struggled. The two that were doing very well were those where he had used a search company to find capable sales leaders and he paid salaries above what he thought was required. Both the finder's fee and the higher salaries were significant but proved to be excellent investments.

In discussions with the board he decided to close down three markets, use recruiters in the remaining markets to find the right quality team, and spend more of his time in these overseas markets supporting them.

Monday reflection

Are you being deliberate and investing enough resources (cash and your time) in your overseas markets? Is it time to shut some down?

Building your leadership team in a new country

In your local market you know how to build your leadership team; you are aware of the exact skills you need for each role as well as the availability and approaches to recruit staff, and the cost is generally known — or at least within a range. In an overseas market this is not the case. Although you know the specific skills for the roles, early on you may need more generalists who can multi-task and respond to challenges and opportunities as they arise, as opposed to subject matter experts in your home market. Also, in an overseas market you may not know the best approaches to recruit staff — which platform or which recruiters are best in your space — and the variability in the cost of people can be significant.

There is no exact formula for success. Below are several suggestions to guide you on how to find leaders in these new markets:

- **Start lean.** A large, expensive team will strain your own, and likely the board's, patience. Keep costs low in the early stages. The higher the costs and the cash burn, the less patience your board will have in continuing operations there.

- **Don't hire a country manager (yet).** Instead, begin with a *business development leader or expansion director,* someone who can grow into the role. When you are starting a new country operation the critical aim is to obtain recurring revenue, so it is logical that the first role should be sales or business development. Target candidates who are one or two levels below the country manager's role in similar industries. They should see this role as an opportunity to prove themselves and then grow into the bigger country manager role.

- **Look for problem-solvers and internal promotions.** You need leaders who are nimble, proactive and think independently. These qualities are hard to validate in interviews, so dive deep in the interviews and into the references, and don't let your urgency create confirmation bias. That means don't just look for the positives, be objectively critical as well. A poor recruiting decision can set your business back 6 to 12 months. Look for candidates with multiple internal promotions within previous companies.

In my career, I have found this to be the greatest predictor of success! Be wary of people who only receive promotions by leaving a company (not within it).

- **Leverage trusted networks.** Use personal connections, reputable search firms and referral-based hiring. Ask existing employees, your network, board, customers and suppliers who they would recommend.

- **Validate their experience in your interviews.** Ask them the same question in multiple ways to test for consistency. Be persistent in your questioning when you sense something in their answer does not quite make sense. I recall doing interviews with a few different people 20 years ago, and they all claimed credit for playing a key role with the iPhone or iPod. Diving deep in the interview and asking them to explain exactly the role they played enables you to confirm their true responsibility and skills, as opposed to what they claim to be the case.

- **Over-invest in interviews.** When hiring a leader for an international expansion, a surface-level interview is not sufficient. You need to invest significant time to assess their values, leadership style and decision making, and also their fit for your business. A structured approach could look like this:

  - **First meeting.** A casual chat over coffee to build rapport, understand their career so far, and get a sense of their personality and values.

  - **Second meeting.** A deeper discussion in your office or over a Zoom call to understand their leadership style, competencies, how they have handled major challenges in previous roles, and how they would approach the role you are offering.

  - **Third meeting.** A dinner setting where you can observe how they interact in a more relaxed environment. I remember taking a country manager candidate out to dinner and my wife, Melinda, came along. At the end of the dinner I asked,

'What did you think?' She replied that he was very good but he would not accept the offer, that there was something aloof about him. She was right. He turned down the offer and used it instead to get a pay rise with his existing employer.

Spending four to five hours across these meetings is the bare minimum to develop confidence in the suitability of a candidate. You're not just hiring for competence, you're hiring for fit, judgement, integrity and alignment with your company's values, and this takes a few conversations for you to evaluate.

- **Undertake extensive reference checking.** Don't rely on the candidate's references. You must reference check with names they did not offer. Leverage your own network to gather unfiltered insights. If using a search firm, ensure they go beyond the candidate's list to validate their reputation with credible industry leaders. Never short-circuit the reference process; it is critical as it will highlight the candidate's true leadership style, their capability, and why they left previous roles.

Connecting and shaping your new leader

Once you have hired the top leader for a country you must invest the time to build a relationship and understanding of how to work together. This will not happen overnight as relationships are a function of time spent together. Below are some suggestions on how to work with this new leader:

- **Invest significant time upfront**. This is especially important in the first six months to build trust, observe their leadership, and ensure they have a deep understanding of your culture. In the first six months, as the founder CEO you should plan to be in market for at least three days each month, spending time with the country manager, building a relationship with them, and understanding how best to work with each other. During this time you will be aligning the leader and their team around your group strategy, and clarifying the country's growth plans. You will also be validating the broader team's capabilities.

- **On critical issues, challenge the leader three times in three different ways.** Their first response may be reflexive or inaccurate. This could occur for many reasons, including that they may not have understood your question. Sometimes, early on, the leader will tell you what they think you want to hear to please you. Therefore, you must press deeper by rephrasing your question or questioning details of their response. Remember the quote 'Trust but verify'.

- **Be on the ground.** When you are in the market, don't just meet with the leader. Engage with employees, have leadership dinners, conduct talent sessions, visit sites, and hold skip-level lunches (as covered in Chapter 3).

- **Spend time with customers.** There is no better market research than visiting customers and discussing the service you are providing. If you have retail or subscriber customers, there are also ways to engage with them, such as through focus groups. Understand first-hand what's working and what isn't in the business. Spending time in the market is necessary and powerful in evaluating how your product is performing in the new country, and why that is the case.

- **Build multiple points of contact.** Don't rely solely on the new leader for information, develop direct relationships with key team members to cross-check insights.

One additional strategic people move: **place a trusted expat in a key leadership role**, ideally as CFO or in a transformation role. While language may be a challenge, this person will serve as both a cultural role model and an objective set of eyes and ears for potential risks to the business. More on this in the following section.

Embedding culture and ensuring compliance

When expanding overseas, cultural alignment will be one of your biggest challenges. In Chapter 4 we discussed how to create a deliberate company culture, now, the stakes are even higher because you are not on the ground to observe and impact the culture. You should have two primary concerns:

1. How do you ensure the new team adopts your company culture?
2. How do you create a culture of compliance?

I have three very sad stories which illustrate the risk of poor compliance. In the first, which was many years ago, we had to fire a whole leadership team — the country manager and all his direct reports — for fraudulent behaviour. In the second situation, I needed to fire the country manager in one of our overseas businesses for bribing customers. He said to me at the time, 'Dane, we are so much better than we were'. My response was, 'Unfortunately, we can't accept any bribery of customers to win contracts'.

And my last example is a very recent one; a business that achieved unicorn valuation status in Southeast Asia, and where they lied about their financial performance. They inflated their revenue and their profit over several years by having two sets of books. I knew these people — in fact, several of them were close friends. So it was very disappointing and upsetting to see the fraudulent behaviour.

The moral of the story is that your company's culture must reject bribery and fraud, even if it is common or tolerated within the country. Sadly, this compliance challenge arises all the time. You must put processes in place to minimise the chance of corruption or fraud.

You should care about this because as founder CEO you have responsibility for every part of the business, in every country in the world. You must work to create a consistent company culture because this is why people join and stay with your company, and you need to be a compliant organisation. Many CEOs have been fired because of corruption in their business, much of which they may not have known about.

To create a consistent culture in this country, use the following approaches:

- **Have a process for onboarding.** Onboarding of all staff, and particularly of leaders, must have specific elements that explain your company's values and culture. Ensure that the leaders understand and can educate their teams on what is, and is not, acceptable in the business.
- **Ensure that you and the leadership team make regular visits, with frequent communication of the company's values.** At a minimum, you or one of your team should visit each month. Use the template in Chapter 4 to identify the actions that will reinforce the company's values, and ensure that those actions are implemented by the country manager and their leadership team.
- **Place home country locals in the business.** They serve the purpose of helping to embed your company's values and culture while also being there to identify potential issues, such as corruption. To add a point to the visits, do all-hands meetings and talk about the company's strategy and values.
- **Follow up with surveys.** Culture, employee engagement, or Employee Net Promoter Score surveys can be useful measures once the business gets to scale.

There are no guarantees to create a compliant business but the initiatives below will increase the probability:

- **Be aware of how you react to bad and good news.** Overreacting can cause leaders to withhold information in the future. Things will go wrong, including compliance issues, key staff departures, major customer losses, or even natural disasters. Your response determines whether people surface problems early or bury them. Pressuring the leader too aggressively may cause the desired result to be achieved in ways that compromise company values or local laws.

- **Create an authority matrix.** This details which decisions need to be made locally versus those that required headquarter approval — either the CFO or you, the founder CEO.
- **Use the grandparent principle for all recruits, for local leaders, including those you interview, for confirming references, packages, etc.** The grandparent principle of approval in business means that a decision or approval must be reviewed and signed off by not just the immediate manager but also their superior (the 'grandparent'). This ensures checks and balances in decision making, reduces bias or favouritism in approval, and adds an extra layer of accountability for key decisions.
- **Ensure that you approve the organisation structure.** Sometimes local leaders will create a convoluted structure to appease or attract a candidate. This structure can then cause problems later.
- **Place an expat, ideally a CFO in the business.** I explained the reasons behind this earlier.
- **Connect with the local team below the country manager.** Do this through team meetings, dinners and skip-level lunches to understand what is happening in the business.
- **Build strong systems, and reporting and auditing approaches.** Standardise the systems to ensure your team can have access to the accounts and the details below the reporting level. Exception-based reporting and analysis are critical. Examples of this could be monthly analysis of revenue reports versus cash receipts, or comparing headcount to the number of pays made.
- **Use a whistle-blower line.** A whistle-blower line is a centralised free phone number that people can call to report issues. There is, of course, the potential for a lot of false complaints from disgruntled employees but that is something you have to accept because there will indeed be issues. In fact, the three examples I went through earlier were all discovered via the whistle-blower lines.

Monday ready

The vision of expanding into international markets is exciting for many reasons. However, the path to achieve success is often massively underestimated — the lead-time to being cash flow positive is generally two to three times longer than forecast. In this chapter you learned about the best approaches to understanding the consumer, the market, and the business dynamics. You heard how to find the right leaders, develop trusting relationships, and develop approaches to ensure a consistent culture and the probability of compliance.

As I have said before, discipline beats vision. Expanding the business overseas is almost every CEO's vision. It is also extremely difficult, but by being a disciplined leader and *deliberately* executing the above practices you will increase your probability of success. Unfortunately, there is no guarantee of success, no matter how good the product or solution is.

Use the key takeaways below to map your targeted changes over the first two months. Focus on only two or three changes this Monday and endeavour to repeat them frequently enough over the next month that they start to become habits. Next month, move onto another two or three changes and again endeavour to demonstrate them frequently.

In the next chapter, I'll show you that as a CEO you need to learn how to lead in a crisis because you will face this, over and over again.

Key takeaways

Grow internationally through proven global approaches.
1. Understand your customers, the market and the business dynamics.
   - Be clear on your value proposition from the outset.
   - Start with a narrow product range and geographic focus.
   - Understand the local competition.
   - Know who your customer is.
   - Scrutinise contracts.

2. Focus on your business model and cost structure.
   - Identify all potential cost levers early.
   - Plan for supplier and distribution failure.
   - Protect your brand.
   - Expect to spend significant time in market.
   - Plan for a long road to cash flow profitability.
3. Find the right leaders.
   - Look for problem solvers.
   - Use trusted networks.
   - Validate their experience with extensive reference checking.
   - Over-invest in interviews and research of candidate.
4. Connect and shape your new leader.
   - Invest significant time upfront and be in the market frequently.
   - Be thoughtful in how you accept good and bad news.
   - Spend time with customers.
   - Build multiple points of contact into the business.
5. Embed culture and ensure compliance.
   - Be aware of how you accept good and bad news.
   - Regularly visit the market.
   - Place a local who you trust in the market.
   - Create an authority matrix and use the grandfather principle.
   - Connect with the local team.
   - Build strong systems and exception-based reporting.
   - Use a whistle-blower line.

CHAPTER 10

Lead through crisis and build resilience

Over my career I've faced significant challenges. One example was when I arranged to meet with a KFC franchisee to shut his stores down for non-payment of royalties over an extended period of time. He came in, sat down and put a handgun on the table. Then said, 'Dane, how are you enjoying living in Johannesburg? Are you feeling safe?' While saying this he was tapping the gun. Then he says 'You have three daughters, don't you — Sophie, Emily and Paige, I think? They are at Dainfern School, right? Are you worried about their safety?' Again, he said this while continuing to tap the gun. That one shook me, but I still shut him down.

I've had to deal with workplace fatalities — an experience that is utterly devastating. I've also faced boardroom conflicts, major corporate crises and multiple restructurings. I was the CEO of a company when its share price dropped by 90 per cent (more on that later).

Early in my career I felt invincible. Stress didn't seem to impact me. But by my late forties it began to affect me and I realised I was not a role model leader. Stress clouded my thinking. I became short-tempered at work and brought those frustrations home. People lost respect for me during that period because I wasn't living my personal or company values because of the pressure. This was a critical turning point; a realisation that resilience isn't just about enduring pressure but managing it effectively and remaining focused on what is most important in the business today and into the future.

As a founder CEO, you will need to learn how to lead in difficult times and under pressure because you will face many crises over your career. Crises are a regular part of business. You need to be consistent in your style of leadership and make good decisions when under stress. You enhance your leadership and your reputation when you do well leading in a crisis, whereas you damage your reputation when you don't exhibit the right values. In this chapter, we will cover:

1. How to lead in times of crisis
2. The seven critical leadership traits
3. The five levers to build grit and resilience
4. Supporting your team through a crisis

How to lead in times of crisis

Crisis is the ultimate test of your leadership. A compelling vision will inspire your team when times are good, but also hold them together when times are tough. Furthermore, in a crisis the stakeholders will look to you for calm, clear and disciplined actions to lead the business back into growth and profitability. As a founder CEO you need to learn how to lead in difficult times because you will face many crises over your career, and the team will be watching you even more intently. Recall the *leadership shadow* concept from Chapter 2.

In a crisis — whether it's the loss of a major customer, a critical team member departure, a brand or reputational issue, or a global shock like COVID-19 — your role as CEO is to lead *deliberately*, to *role-model* how you want the rest of your team to lead, and to maintain focus on what matters in this moment but with an eye on the future. This is when your behaviours matter most because your leadership is very intently watched and evaluated in this situation.

When leading in crisis, most of your leadership behaviours should be the same as when there is no crisis — this is because at all times you must lead the business with urgency. A quote from Andy Pearson, prior

CEO of the consulting firm McKinsey & Co., former Dean of Harvard Business School and former Chairman of Yum! Brands, is 'Even when the business is ten per cent up, run it like it is ten per cent down!'

The team is evaluating you to see how you respond in these difficult times and the questions they will be considering are:

- **Are you a person of hope?** Does the team have confidence in your ability to lead them through this crisis?
- **Are you in control?** Does the team see you calmly evaluating the situation, handling the pressure and identifying solutions?
- **Do you have a coherent plan to work through the issues while anticipating what could come next?** I love the quote, 'Hope for the best, but plan for the worst'. Is that how you are leading?
- **Are you behaving in a way that is consistent with your company values?** It is most difficult to uphold company values when under stress. However, this is when your behaviour and your company's values are on the most visible display.

We are all human, and crises affect us. It's okay to feel the pressure and momentarily dip. This could be evident in your visible frustration or disappointment with an outcome, but you need to bounce back quickly. This chapter provides guidance and insights on how to lead in crisis and deliberately build resilience.

The connection between crisis and grief

A business crisis is remarkably similar to experiencing loss. Grief is a natural reaction. Any crisis — whether it's losing funding, a key employee, a major client, or, as we saw in 2020, navigating a global pandemic — feels like loss. Crises trigger emotional responses like grief. Let me explain by sharing the Kübler-Ross Model of Grief.

Elisabeth Kübler-Ross was a Swiss-American psychiatrist best known for her work on the psychological process of dying and grief. In her 1969 book *On Death and Dying*, she introduced the Kübler-Ross model, which describes the five stages of grief. These stages were originally based on her work with terminally ill patients but have since been widely applied to various forms of loss, including bereavement, job loss, divorce and other life changes.

The Five Stages of Grief (Kübler-Ross model)

1. **Denial:** A defence mechanism where individuals refuse to accept the reality of loss. It helps cushion the initial shock. *Example:* 'This can't be happening'.
2. **Anger:** As denial fades, frustration and resentment emerge, often directed at oneself, others, or the situation. *Example:* 'Why is this happening to me? Who is to blame?'
3. **Bargaining:** Attempting to regain control by making deals or promises, often with a higher power. *Example:* 'If I do this, maybe things will change'.
4. **Depression:** Deep sadness and despair set in as the reality of loss becomes unavoidable. *Example:* 'What's the point of going on?'
5. **Acceptance:** Coming to terms with the loss and moving forward. *Example:* 'I can't change this, but I can adjust'.
6. Later, **'meaning'** was added. Being inspired to make a difference based on the experience that you have just been through. *Example:* My father passed away from colon cancer, so now I am very active in driving awareness and the need for people to have colonoscopies.

Kübler-Ross's research is highly relevant in understanding human responses to adversity, crisis and even change. Though originally developed based on research of people with life-threatening illnesses, these stages apply to business crises as well. Recognising this will help you manage your own emotions and support your team effectively.

This is a crucial concept. When you acknowledge what you're going through and understand it is a normal journey, it can give you confidence to know that you will emerge at the other end, even if it is painful. Understanding your team's journey through these stages also allows you to lead with empathy, in that you understand how they are feeling, and confident, in that you know that they are moving through the stages of grief, and this is normal.

Proven methods exist for managing stress and handling crises objectively. I'll share these later in the chapter.

You might think, 'Stress doesn't affect me. I'm not an emotional person. Business is business'. Maybe that's true today, and maybe crises seem rare. However, over time, stress accumulates.

Think of it like physical fatigue. One intense workout is fine, but constant overexertion without recovery leads to injury. Stress accumulates the same way. The more you endure, the more it affects you — whether through anxiety, lack of sleep, frustration with your team, or strain on personal relationships. That's why learning to lead under stress is essential. Later in the chapter, we'll explore how to manage stress effectively. But for now, let's focus on your key actions as a leader in crisis.

The seven critical leadership traits

All of the leadership traits we identified in Chapter 2 still apply, but these seven are especially critical in a crisis:

1. Be aware of your leadership shadow. (I reference this in every chapter because it's that important.)
2. Be a person of hope and a simplifier.
3. Be visible and out front.
4. Know the details intimately.
5. Get close to the front line.
6. Focus on less to achieve more.
7. Reinforce company values through leadership.

Here's a deeper dive into the leadership behaviours that you need to be *deliberate* in their use in times of crisis:

1. **Be aware of your leadership shadow.** Times of crisis magnify your leadership shadow as the team watches you even more closely. Long after the crisis, people will remember whether your decisions were fair and respectful, and consistent with the company values.

2. **Be a person of hope and a simplifier.** The team needs someone who is confident about the future but also pragmatic about current realities. You must cut through the noise, communicating clear perspectives of the current situation while laying out the roadmap to take the business forward.

3. **Be out front, visible and communicate with the team.** In times of crisis, the team is looking for you. Think about the president or prime minister of a country. When there is a crisis in the country, the media love to find out the leader was nowhere to be seen, or worse still, at some holiday resort. You need to keep the team informed; and remember, it is impossible to over-communicate. Increase your engagement with frequent all-hands meetings. If you currently hold them bi-weekly or monthly, switch to weekly updates. Keep the team informed about business developments and celebrate small wins. Step in and take ownership of significant issues. Your presence reassures the team.

4. **Know the details intimately.** Step above the chaos but also understand the specifics. In times of crisis, superficial knowledge isn't enough. Ask yourself:
   - What is most important right now?
   - What am I missing?
   - Is my team being fully honest, or are they telling me what they think I want to hear?
   - Am I being too optimistic (recall the Introduction and founders' optimism trap)? How could this crisis unfold?
   - What are the best- and worst-case outcomes?

- Which stakeholders need to be updated — banks, investors, the board, your family? Talk to all the stakeholders involved to find out which ones are or are not in crisis. During the COVID-19 pandemic, everyone was in crisis. That's unique. Usually, in a crisis, only a few stakeholders are in crisis. Understand who is in crisis, what role you can play to support them and, more importantly, who can support you.
- Am I hoping for the best but planning for the worst?

5. **Get close to the front line.** Information flowing through multiple levels in an organisation can be slow and affect the accuracy of this information. Get close to the front line to understand exactly what is happening. That puts you in a better position, you get information more quickly and accurately, and therefore you can make quicker decisions and implement changes faster. Speed and accuracy in crisis management can mean the difference between minor setbacks and major failures.

6. **Focus on less to achieve more.** What is important right now? It's almost always about cash flow. What are the three or four levers you can pull to help that situation? For example, growing the business uses cash, so you might dial back your sales and business development initiatives to conserve cash. Think, 'What else can we stop doing?' Sales and business development are good examples, but what other controllable investments can you reduce (such as tighter inventory management)? Be ruthless in your prioritisation; every minute and dollar spent on non-essential efforts in a crisis puts your business further at risk.

7. **Emphasise your company values.** We spoke in Chapter 4 about the importance of your values. They are a filter by which you make decisions. In a crisis, regularly challenge yourself and your team to ensure that your actions align with those values. If transparency is one of your values, tell your stakeholders as much as you can without increasing uncertainty. Sometimes, too much information can fuel confusion and fear rather than reduce it.

Founder story

Emily was the founder of a medical products startup. While she was on Christmas leave and overseas on holiday, her company had a malware attack that froze all the operational and financial systems. Fortunately, the business was shut down anyway for the Christmas break so the impact was minimal at the time. She also had a very competent CTO who had a plan of attack to resolve the issue.

Recognising the importance of her presence to the team, she immediately flew back home to be with them as they worked through the issues. She was in constant communication with the CTO and the broader team, giving them all confidence that the situation would be resolved quickly.

Monday reflection

When there is a crisis, do you step in to be that person of hope, and to be out front and visible? If your business is now in a challenging time, what can you do differently to be a person of hope?

A final thought ties back to the Kübler-Ross model. Acknowledge the stage of grief you are in. Are you in denial? Are you being too optimistic? Remember, hope for the best, plan for the worst. An approach to protect you from this situation is to appoint someone on your team to be a devil's advocate to challenge your thinking. This person should ask tough questions, stress-test your assumptions, and force you to consider worst-case scenarios. It's not a fun role, but it is an essential one.

The five levers to build grit and resilience

Recall that disciplined leaders are *deliberate, self-aware, role models* and *relentless students.* To be able to demonstrate all these behaviours, even in times of crisis, leaders need both grit and resilience.

Grit is a proactive word. It a mindset and an action to keep pushing ahead despite difficulties and roadblocks. In some ways it is easier to achieve than resilience because it is a decision that you make to drive forward. Resilience is the ability to withstand adversity and keep bouncing back. It is only developed and accumulated over time through experiencing and getting through crises. Resilience is confidence you build in yourself in overcoming adversity, time and time again.

You must be deliberate about how you build both grit and resilience. The five levers can help guide you on this journey:

1. Have a powerful purpose.
2. Build awareness and learn how to reset.
3. Accept uncertainty.
4. Become comfortable handling conflict.
5. Exhibit self-care.

Let me share a story of my experience with grit and resilience. I was a CEO of a company when the share price dropped by 90 per cent. This was the worst time in the wine industry's history. There was a massive oversupply within Australia and the industry was producing 30 per cent more wine than it could sell. Our company was producing 50 per cent more wine than we had a home for in our brands. Wine at the medium-to-low price range is a commodity, so prices were significantly down. On top of that, Australia was experiencing the worst drought in its history, forcing up the cost of buying water for irrigation of vineyards.

Retailer consolidation was also putting immense pressure on wine companies. The Australian currency was at a 20-year high, making exports expensive. Given that Australia exported about 60 per cent of its wine, and our company exported 70 per cent, our products became much harder to sell internationally.

Our company also had some structural problems that I inherited, including a contractual obligation to buy grapes at a price that was above market rates. Every day we fought to keep the company afloat. By the time I left, we had increased the share price five-fold from its lowest point.

My wife asked me one morning, 'How do you get out of bed? Every day is a crisis'. My answer was always the same, 'I need to for the 3000 team members who rely on me in this business'. Most CEOs feel the same obligation to their teams and customers in times of crisis.

Leaders need both grit and resilience. By using the levers in this section, you will build these qualities. These are practical tools and approaches that can help you withstand crises and challenges.

You might think, 'I can rely on my team or external consultants during these challenging times', or 'If I focus on growth, I can grow my way out of this'. Both approaches have merit; however, the crisis may prevent you from relying on these solutions alone. Growing the business consumes cash, and that may be your biggest problem.

The five levers to building grit and resilience are listed below.

Lever 1: Have a powerful purpose

Grit comes from having a compelling reason to push through adversity, to keep moving the business forward. This is the motivation to keep going. For most founders, the driver is a combination of your product or service which supports customers in a unique and impactful way, your sense of obligation to your employees and their families, and your obligation to your shareholders, many of whom are likely family and friends who were your initial investors.

The above list may be your drivers to push ahead but the organisation needs a compelling purpose to align the team right next to you.

Recall that in Chapter 4 we covered building a deliberate culture, and the need to have a vision and purpose for your company. If your company does not have a purpose yet, Lever 1 is another catalyst for you to create it *on Monday.*

Lever 2: Build awareness and learn how to reset

Earlier, we explored the Kübler-Ross framework of grief. Use that. Consider your position on that curve. Think about where your team is. Think about where your customers may be. That awareness can help you lead more effectively, as you know where they are emotionally and what they may need from you to move forward.

Recall that in Chapter 3 we covered how important emotional intelligence is in building trust, and I shared world-renowned expert and author on emotional intelligence Daniel Goleman's insights on skills that contribute to greater emotional intelligence. Two of these are also critical skills for you to build grit and resilience by understanding how stress is affecting you.

Self-awareness

- Emotional self-awareness is the ability to read and understand your emotions as well as recognise their impact on work performance, relationships and the like.
- Accurate self-assessment is a realistic evaluation of your strengths and limitations in normal business times, and in times of crisis.
- This is a critical insight for you to utilise in times of crisis as you reflect on how well you are handling the pressure, how well you respond to different situations, how the team is responding to the crisis and how you are leading.

Self-management

- Self-control is the ability to keep disruptive emotions and impulses under control, and to be deliberate and manage your response.

- We all get triggered, and more often when under stress. A trigger leads to an emotion, which leads to a behaviour. A trigger could be a board meeting or a phone call from a difficult customer that makes you anxious and puts stress on you. Be aware of your triggers but also be mindful of how to use the gap between the trigger and your response. Use that gap to make a deliberate action that will help the situation, not aggravate it.

In his book *The Third Space*, Adam Fraser talks about the space between two events. An example for me is the transition between work and home. I used to drive home from work and often received phone calls at 6 or 7 pm. I don't know about you, but I've never received good news at that hour. It is always a bad news call. I would finish the call and go into the house, calling out a greeting to my family as I walked up the stairs. I would then go to my study or bedroom, unpack my gym gear from the morning (I'm a gym junkie), have a shower, and come downstairs 10–15 minutes later, clear-headed and ready for the family. That brief reset allowed me to show up better for my family rather than bringing home the stress of the day.

Founder story

Sarah was a talented athlete at school and university. Immediately after university she launched her startup, and after six years the business was doing well with good sales growth and was cash-flow positive. However, Sarah was constantly stressed, working 14 hours a day with no time for anything else. Or that is what she felt to be the case, as she felt guilty about doing anything other than working on the business.

In our discussions, we identified that exercise had always been her stress relief and she had stopped it completely. Over six months

---

she gradually developed a routine, increased her fitness, and retrained herself to start her day at 5.30 am which was 'frictionless time' for her, when no-one needed her, and she could dedicate time and mind space to her exercise.

Monday reflection

What is your third space to reset? Are you using it frequently enough?

You need to find your third space, too. It might be five deep breaths between phone calls or Zoom meetings so you're not carrying negative energy from one conversation to the next. It could be walking to the kitchen to get a cup of coffee. With each new meeting, the team is observing you to gauge what mood you are in. Slight pauses create space for you to reset your emotions and diffuse the stress from the prior situation, positioning you to make unemotional decisions and be more deliberate in your leadership as you move onto the next issue.

Lever 3: Accept uncertainty

Working in the wine industry taught me how to lead in an industry of uncertainty. So much of that business's P&L was out of our control, from the weather's impact on grape quality, yield and cost; to the cost of other important inputs such as water for irrigation; and the impact of the Australian dollar on our ability to be competitive and successful in selling into international markets.

All companies and industries have some uncertainty, and as a leader you must learn to make decisions with varying amounts of information. This comes with experience and your confidence to trust your judgement in the absence of complete information. In times of crisis, the speed of decision making can be critical, so having the confidence to make a quick decision in times of uncertainty is a necessary skill.

Regret can be an emotion that undermines your ability to make quick decisions and to build resilience. When you reflect on past decisions, the wins and the mistakes, consider what you have learned and how to apply those learnings. This is a far more productive approach than thinking, 'I should have done [... ...], instead of the decision I made', and having that thought undermine your confidence going forward.

Lever 4: Be comfortable handling conflict

Go back to Chapter 3 and review the components about handling conflict. As a founder CEO you handle conflict many times a day, whether or not the business is in crisis.

Develop comfort in addressing conflict; having difficult and challenging conversations without emotion will reduce your stress. This only comes from practice. Over time, you learn to accept that conflict is inevitable and you can manage through it to achieve an acceptable outcome, without it emotionally impacting you.

Lever 5: Exhibit self-care

I love the expression from airline safety demonstrations: 'Put your own oxygen mask on first'. As a founder CEO, it's okay to be a bit selfish. Think about how you take care of yourself. Maybe that means acknowledging, 'I know I could work all night, but I need four or five hours of sleep, so I'm going home to rest'.

Clinical studies prove that exercise reduces stress and promotes relaxation; make time for it, even when you feel you don't have enough time. Maybe it's not your usual 60-minute gym routine but instead a 15-to-20-minute run.

Throughout my career, I have always found time to exercise five or six times a week. This routine and the endurance it created, has assisted my ability to keep going through adversity.

Supporting your team through a crisis

In uncertain times, many leaders instinctively consolidate decision making at the top. Times of crisis often require the opposite approach. You must empower teams to tackle different challenges simultaneously.

Create a forum where rapid debate can take place. Be clear: everyone has a voice, but not always a vote. You, as the founder CEO, must be decisive and make the final decision.

These crisis-response teams may look different from your usual leadership teams. Choose leaders based on:

- **Experience.** They've handled crises before and know how to navigate uncertainty.
- **Temperament.** They remain calm and in control under pressure.
- **Mindset.** They balance optimism with pragmatism, acknowledging risks while driving solutions.
- **Agility.** They can think quickly, adapt to evolving situations, and make tough calls with incomplete information.

Put rotations and systems in place to keep people fresh. If your business operates 24/7 or is located across a number of time zones, ensure that leadership coverage is well-distributed. You should not expect any single individual, including yourself, to function at full capacity around the clock.

During crises, clarity is critical. Everyone must understand their role, responsibilities, and decision-making authority. Define:

- What decisions can individuals make independently?
- What must be escalated to you?
- What decisions do you need to involve the board or investors in?

Set up welfare checks to monitor team members under extreme stress. Their behaviour will probably change under pressure, and those struggling the most will need additional support.

Adjusting incentives to drive the right behaviour

Consider if your current incentive system aligns with crisis priorities. This is a tough decision when the business is haemorrhaging cash. However, remember the quote from Chapter 4: 'What gets measured, and bonused, gets done'.

Think about adjusting incentives to focus on the key actions that will stabilise and ultimately turn the business around. Short-term sacrifices may be necessary, but if your team members understand the long-term vision, they will be more willing to make those trade-offs.

If you lack confidence in your teams because of limited crisis experience, conduct frequent check-ins on their decision making. This ensures that they stay aligned with your company priorities and adapt their approach as needed.

Monday ready

In this chapter, you've learned that as a CEO, you will inevitably face many crises. Your vision plays an important role, even when the business is in crisis, as it remains the aspirational destination that you and the team continue to drive towards. However, it is disciplined leadership that is the way out of the crisis. You must be *deliberate* in your actions, you are being watched intently so *role modelling* is critical, and the skill of being a *relentless student* will assist you if you have seen this issue before, or this may be a difficult but powerful lesson to assist you in the future.

Remember the *leadership shadow* concept from Chapter 2. Your team will take cues from how you handle pressure. You are human, and stress will affect you. Don't assume you are immune to stress. It might not hit you immediately, but it will over time. And don't pretend everything is fine when it's not. It's okay to share how you're feeling with the right people. Authenticity builds trust, and trust fuels resilience.

Refer to the below list of key takeaways and reflect which of these may be most relevant for you given where your business is today. When future crises arise (which they will) refer back to this list for guidance.

Key takeaways

Lead through crisis and build resilience.
1. Seven critical leadership traits to exhibit in times of crisis.
    - Be aware of your leadership shadow.
    - Be a person of hope and simplifier.
    - Be visible and out front.
    - Know the details intimately.
    - Get close to the front line.

- Focus on less to achieve more.
- Reinforce company values through leadership.
2. Five levers to build grit and resilience.
   - Have a powerful purpose.
   - Build awareness and learn how to reset.
   - Accept uncertainty.
   - Become comfortable handling conflict.
   - Exhibit self-care.
3. Support your team.
   - Choose leaders based on experience, temperament, mindset and agility.
   - Does everyone understand their role, responsibilities, and decision-making authority?
   - Rotate your team to support them.
   - Put in the right incentives.

Conclusion: Monday relaunch

To be a successful leader, in business or life, requires having an aspirational vision of your target destination. This could be an outstanding product, service or solution your business provides to customers. It could be a market share or financial goal. It may be an outcome you target to achieve for your community or philanthropic organisation, or for your sporting team or for your family.

Having a vision is critical! Most people push ahead with greater energy and persistence, when you have something to strive for.

However, discipline beats vision!

Recall that disciplined leaders are deliberate, self-aware, and consistently role-model the behaviours they expect from others. They are relentless students, constantly evolving their leadership approaches and reinventing themselves as new challenges arise or as the business requires.

Every action and behaviour by you will lead to a specific and predictable response by your team and those you interact with. I have stated multiple times already that 'For every action, there's an equal and opposite reaction' (Newton's Third Law of Motion). Leadership works exactly the same way. Being disciplined in your leadership behaviours creates discipline in your team and organisation.

This discipline builds trust and a high level of accountability by your team, a better relationship with your board and investors, and a stronger business. Discipline will also help your personal life. You will build deeper relationships with the people you care about, and in turn, they will provide you with the support you need to succeed. Discipline will enable you to better handle stress through building resilience to the inevitable business and life challenges. All this will lead to better balance in your life, while also building a substantial business, including higher revenue, greater profit and an increased valuation.

The changes suggested in this book may seem challenging, and even unnatural and inauthentic to start. You will find though, that over time, these new disciplined leadership behaviours become habits for you. Once this occurs, being an authentic leader becomes a bit easier.

This book has given you the tools to achieve success in business and, importantly, in life. Scaling a company is thrilling but chaotic and stressful, and the difference between success and failure is more than the vision or the attractiveness of your product or service. It is your disciplined leadership.

Use this handbook as a roadmap. Each chapter covers a critical element in the journey to become a disciplined and impactful leader. Frequently refer to the appropriate chapters until you feel you are as competent as you need to be. If you feel some old habits creeping back in, which can occur under stress, go back and refresh these disciplines. Identify someone in your team who can be an observer and provide you feedback if your *leadership shadow* is neutral or negative as opposed to positive and motivating for the team. Yes, I've mentioned leadership shadow in every chapter, and now again, in the conclusion. If this concept confuses you, please refer to Chapter 2, as it is the most important leadership lever you have.

No matter how strong you are as a leader, there is significant luck and timing in business which can ultimately determine whether the business is successful or not. However, discipline will significantly increase the probability of you achieving the results you want.

The practices and ideas in this book, if implemented, will make you a good leader. You can only become an outstanding leader through practice and being a *relentless student*. Remember, your life journey is your leadership journey. To become an outstanding leader, you must become a student of leadership. Invest the time in identifying, observing and reflecting on what you see in other leaders and then evolving your own leadership style.

The return on investment will be high, financially and personally. In developing discipline, you give your startup its best chance of success, and you will reap a financial reward for that. And discipline will keep you and those you love happy. Your upfront time investment will yield many future rewards.

My hope is that thousands of founder CEOs will read this book (I cannot mentor them all), sparking a massive wave of change in how new companies are led with discipline and, thereby, improving their chances of success.

In this book I share all my secrets and strategies. That said, most founder CEOs need a mentor: someone to talk to when times get tough and chaotic, and even someone to celebrate the wins with. That is what I do. I mentor CEOs to apply these ideas and become disciplined, impactful leaders. If the concepts in this book resonate with you, perhaps I can help. Connect with me on LinkedIn or refer to my website (www.impactfulleadership.com).

You will become a disciplined leader if you follow the practices in this book. And then you will become an *impactful leader*. It's a lot of work, I know, but you have a lot at stake. And you can be sure of a high return on the investment you make, starting Monday.